센치한 Listening 길들이기

감성 맞춤 내신 공략

센치한 LISTENING 길들이기 마무리 2

출판일　　｜1판 1쇄 발행 2014년 8월 29일

지은이　　｜김민주, William Winchester
펴낸이　　｜최회영
책임편집　｜김소연, 이수미
영문교열　｜이윤선, 윤은지, 강소영, Peggy Anderson
디자인　　｜성윤지, 노영남, 이보람
펴낸곳　　｜(주)컴퍼스미디어
출판신고　｜1980년 3월 29일 제 406-2007-00046 ⓒ ㈜ 웅진씽크빅 2011
주소　　　｜서울특별시 서초구 서초2동 1360-31 정진빌딩 3층
전화　　　｜(02)3471- 0096
홈페이지　｜http://www.compasspub.com
ISBN　　 ｜978-89-6697-785-7

이 책의 구성과 특징

01 Introduction

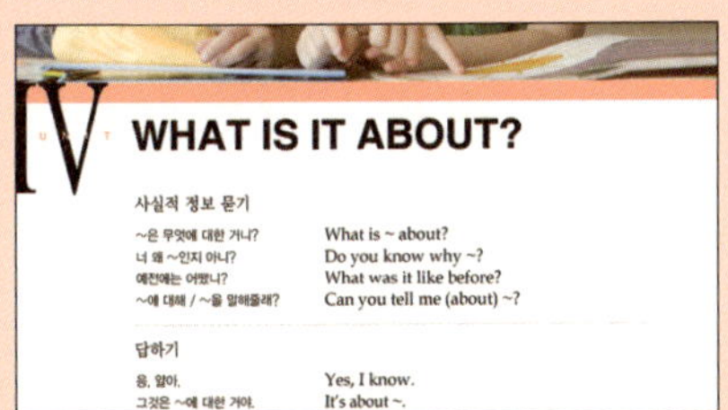

Unit에서 학습의 초점이 되는 주요 의사소통 기능과 예문들을 먼저 학습합니다.

02 Words

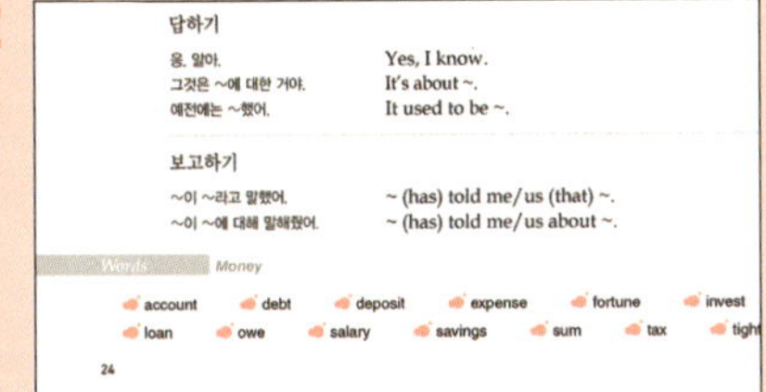

듣기평가에서 자주 출제되는 특정 주제의 중요 어휘를 익힙니다.

03 Check Up

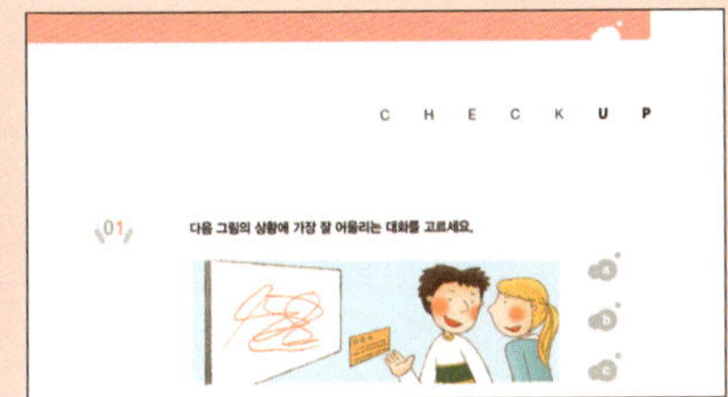

01–02. 앞서 배운 의사소통 기능을 중심으로 구성된 짧은 내용을 듣고, 간단한 연습 문제를 풀어봅니다.

03. 빈칸에 알맞은 의사소통 표현을 써 보면서 해당 표현들을 확실히 기억합니다.

04 Actual Test

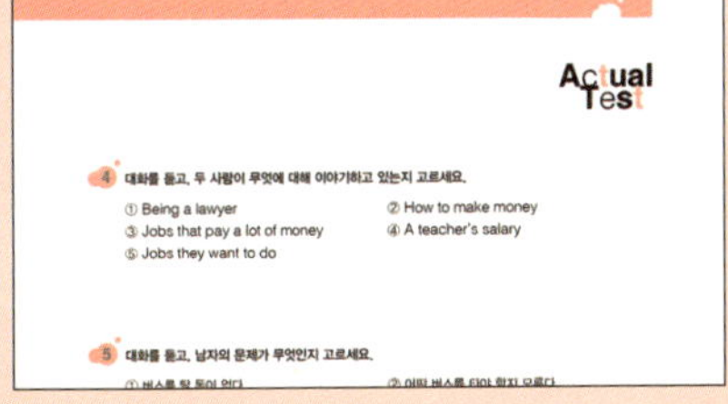

핵심 의사소통 기능을 포함한 내용으로 구성된 8문항의 문제를 풀어봅니다. 다양한 유형의 실전 듣기평가 문제 유형을 익힐 수 있습니다.

05 Dictation

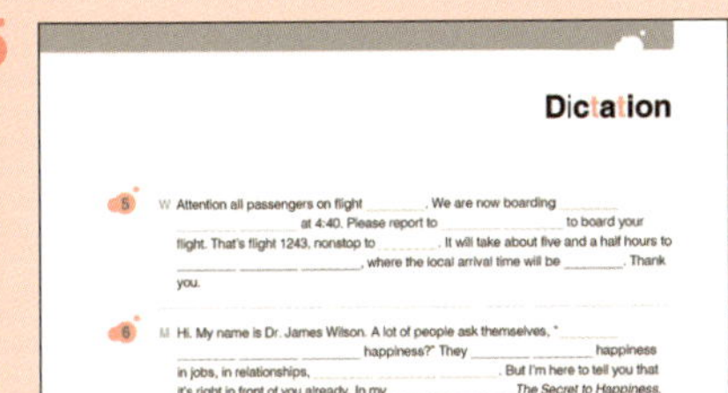

Actual Test 8문항의 스크립트를 다시 듣고 빈칸을 채우면서 주요 표현과 어휘를 복습합니다.

06 모의고사

실전과 똑같은 스타일로 구성된 총 3회의 모의고사를 통해 실제 듣기평가 시험에 완벽 대비합니다.

Table of Contents

이 책의 구성과 특징   3

UNIT I   WHAT SHOULD I DO?   6

UNIT II   WHAT DO YOU LIKE TO DO FOR FUN?   12

UNIT III   WHERE CAN I FIND THE POST OFFICE?   18

UNIT IV   WHAT IS IT ABOUT?   24

UNIT V   DO YOU MIND IF WE TALK ABOUT IT?   30

UNIT VI   DO YOU REMEMBER?   36

UNIT VII   ARE YOU SURE?   42

UNIT VIII   **GUESS WHAT!**   **48**

UNIT IX   **YOU'RE SUPPOSED TO BE CAREFUL.**   **54**

UNIT X   **I'LL KEEP THAT IN MIND.**   **60**

UNIT XI   **HAVE YOU EVER BEEN ON A DIET?**   **66**

UNIT XII   **WHAT WOULD YOU DO IF YOU WERE PRESIDENT?**   **72**

별책 부록

모의고사 1회

모의고사 2회

모의고사 3회

정답 및 해설

A Separate-Volume Supplement : Answers and Audio scripts . MP3 File CD

I WHAT SHOULD I DO?

충고 · 조언 요구하기

(그 일을) 어떻게 해야 하지?	What should I do (with it)?
내가 ~해야 한다고 생각해?	Do you think I should ~?
(~에 대해서) 조언 좀 해줄 수 있어?	Could you give me some tips (on ~)?
네가 ~한다면 어떻게 하겠니?	What would you do if you ~?

충고 · 조언하기

넌 ~하는/하지 않는 것이 좋겠어.	You'd better (not) ~.
네가 ~하는 것을 권해.	I suggest (that) you (should) ~.
	I suggest/recommend -ing ~.
~하지 그래?	Why don't you ~?
내 생각엔 네가 ~해야 할 것 같아.	I think you should ~.
나라면 ~하겠어.	I would ~.

Words   **Animals & Plants**

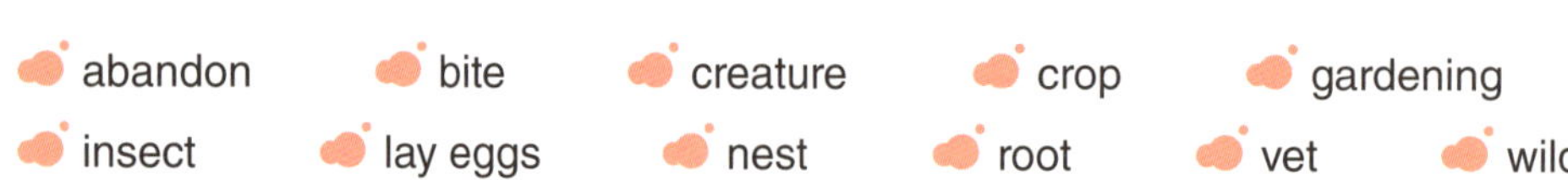

- abandon
- bite
- creature
- crop
- gardening
- insect
- lay eggs
- nest
- root
- vet
- wild

01 대화를 듣고, 두 사람이 이야기하고 있는 강아지를 고르세요.

02 대화를 듣고, 내용과 일치하면 T, 일치하지 않으면 F에 ✓ 표 하세요.

1 The girl is going to her grandfather's farm. [T] [F]

2 The boy is going away for the summer. [T] [F]

3 The grandfather grows corn on his farm. [T] [F]

03 주어진 표현을 사용하여 대화를 완성하세요.

Do you think I should	Why don't you
I suggest that you	Could you give me some tips

A I'm thinking about planting a garden. _________________ do it?

B Sure. I have one, and it's a great hobby. _________________ try it.

A OK. _________________ on starting a garden?

B _________________ read a few books about gardening first?

들려주는 내용을 잘 듣고 물음에 답하세요.

1 여자가 할 일로 언급되지 <u>않은</u> 것을 고르세요.

①  ②  ③  ④  ⑤ 

2 대화를 듣고, 여자가 남자에게 조언한 것을 고르세요.

① 연극에 출연하지 말 것 ② 연기에 집중할 것

③ 대사를 잊어버리지 말 것 ④ 관객의 반응을 살필 것

⑤ 연극을 보러 올 것

3 다음을 듣고, 글의 종류로 가장 적절한 것을 고르세요.

① speech ② announcement ③ advertisement

④ news report ⑤ letter

4 대화를 듣고, 남자의 문제가 무엇인지 고르세요.

① He needs to visit a doctor.

② He doesn't have money for the vet.

③ His pet cat recently died.

④ He hasn't been sleeping or eating.

⑤ His cat is too aggressive.

5 대화를 듣고, 상황을 가장 잘 나타낸 문장을 고르세요.

① The man found baby birds in his yard.　② The woman wants to keep the bird eggs.
③ The man found a bird's nest with eggs.　④ The woman wants a bird for a pet.
⑤ The man raises lots of baby birds.

6 대화를 듣고, 아래 포스터에서 <u>잘못된</u> 것을 고르세요.

7 대화를 듣고, 남자가 여자에게 권한 것을 고르세요.

① 모기향 피우기　　　　　　　　　② 벌레 물린 곳에 약 바르기
③ 벌레 퇴치 스프레이 뿌리기　　　　④ 텐트에 모기장 설치하기
⑤ 벌레에 신경 쓰지 않기

8 다음 짝지어진 대화 중 <u>어색한</u> 것을 고르세요.

①　　　　　　②　　　　　　③　　　　　　④　　　　　　⑤

다음을 듣고 빈칸에 들어갈 알맞은 말을 쓰세요.

1

M　What are you doing today, Layla? I thought we might _________ _________ _________.

W　I have some _________ _________ _________. I have to go to the gym, for one.

M　That shouldn't take long. _________ _________ are you doing?

W　After that I have to mail a few letters at the post office. Then I'm doing some grocery shopping.

M　OK. Can we meet after that?

W　Almost. I just have to _________ _________ my dry cleaning first.

M　OK. Why don't you just _________ _________ _________ _________ when you're done?

2

M　Are you coming to the play tonight? I have _________ _________ _________.

W　Congratulations! That must be exciting.

M　Yes, but I'm a little nervous. Do you _________ _________ _________?

W　I suggest you don't worry _________ _________ _________.

M　What do you mean?

W　Just _________ _________ your performance. You'll be fine!

M　Thanks for _________ _________, Rose.

W　Sure. I'll see you at the play tonight.

3

W　Today in Chicago, a bear _________ _________ the city zoo. So far, it has not been seen by anyone in the city. Workers from the zoo say that the bear is very _________. They _________ that you stay far away from the bear. And if you do see it, call the police. Above all, do not _________ the wild animal for any reason. We'll bring you more information as the story develops.

4

M　My cat has been really sick lately.

W　Really? _________ _________ with him?

M　Well, he is tired _________ _________ _________. And he isn't eating.

W　_________ _________ _________ take him to the vet?

M　I'm not sure if I can afford _________ _________ _________.

W　It can be expensive. But isn't it _________ _________ for your cat?

M　Well, he is my best friend. Maybe I can work a little extra to pay the bill.

W　_________ _________, you'll be glad you did it when he's well again.

M　You're right. Thanks for the talk, Gina.

5

W What is that you have there, Mike?

M It's a __________ __________. I found it in my backyard last night.

W Oh, it must have __________ __________ __________ __________.

M Yeah. __________ __________, it had two small eggs in it.

W Why would a mother bird __________ __________ and then abandon them?

M I don't think it did. Maybe it got hurt or died.

W That could be. __________ __________ take good care of those eggs.

6

M I can't wait for the City Arts Festival on Saturday.

W I know; it's going to be great. We'll get to speak __________ __________ __________.

M Yeah. I'm thinking of entering the __________ __________, too. Should I do it?

W I really __________ __________ __________. Your paintings are really good.

M Thanks. I'll bring __________ __________ __________. Where do you want to meet?

W I'll meet you at City Plaza, __________ __________ __________ __________.

M OK. I'll be __________ __________ __________ when the festival starts at 11:00.

7

M Is this your __________ __________ camping, Molly?

W Yes. I'm having __________ __________ __________ __________, though.

M Me too. I do wish there were __________ __________.

W Yeah, they're __________ __________, especially when they bite.

M I have some __________ for that, if you need it.

W That would be great. How do I use it?

M __________ __________ __________ it on your arms and legs. It will __________ the bugs __________.

W Thanks, Jim! I'll do that right away.

8

① M How do I __________ __________ __________ all these weeds?

   W I suggest you __________ __________ __________ by the roots.

② M How should I study for my English test?

   W I __________ using note cards.

③ M What should I do with this old food?

   W No, you relax __________ __________ __________ dinner.

④ M __________ __________ __________ I should try out for the team?

   W Yes, I think you would have fun.

⑤ M __________ __________ __________ come to the movies with us?

   W That sounds great. I need to __________ __________ __________.

UNIT II WHAT DO YOU LIKE TO DO FOR FUN?

관심 묻기

너는 한가할 때 뭘 하는 걸 좋아하니?	What do you enjoy (doing) in your free time?
너는 뭘 하는 걸 좋아하니?	What do you like doing/to do?
너는 ~에 관심이 있니?	Are you interested in ~?
너는 ~하는 걸 좋아하니?	Do you enjoy/like ~?

관심 말하기

나는 ~하는 것을 좋아해.	I enjoy/like ~.
나는 ~에 관심이 있어.	I'm interested in ~. / I have an interest in ~.
나는 ~을 아주 좋아해.	I'm fond of ~. / I'm keen on ~.
나는 ~에 관심이 없어.	I'm not interested in ~.

Words   *Hobbies*

 climb    hit the slopes    interest   keen   magazine   novel

passion   take up   tour   voluntary

01 대화를 듣고, 여자가 친구들과 하기 좋아하는 것을 고르세요.

02 대화를 듣고, 해당하는 것에 ✓ 표 하세요.

	Coins	Comic Books
Can be worth more money		
Can provide fun		
Are all unique		

03 주어진 표현을 사용하여 대화를 완성하세요.

What do you like	I'm interested in	I enjoy	in your free time

A Hi, Beth. _________________ to do for fun?

B Oh, _________________ reading novels. What do you enjoy doing
_________________?

A _________________ literature as well. What's your favorite book?

B My favorite book is *The Great Gatsby*.

들려주는 내용을 잘 듣고 물음에 답하세요.

1 대화를 듣고, 두 사람이 토요일에 할 일을 고르세요.

① 역사 투어 참가하기
② 도서관에서 공부하기
③ 역사 수업 보고서 쓰기
④ 역사 박물관 관람 예약하기
⑤ 역사에 대한 다큐멘터리 보기

2 대화를 듣고, 여자의 마지막 말에 대한 남자의 응답으로 가장 적절한 것을 고르세요.

M

① Sure, I will definitely come.
② No, I have other plans.
③ No, I don't like geology.
④ Yes, I will if I can.
⑤ Yes, geology is my favorite.

3 대화를 듣고, 두 사람이 만날 시각을 고르세요.

① 8:00　　② 9:00　　③ 10:00　　④ 11:00　　⑤ 12:00

4 다음을 듣고, 남자의 직업을 고르세요.

① car designer
② magazine writer
③ car mechanic
④ race car driver
⑤ car collector

5 대화를 듣고, 여자가 남자에게 전화를 건 목적을 고르세요.

① 등산 모임에 초대하려고
② 등산에 대해 물어보려고
③ 등산용품 가게의 위치를 물어보려고
④ 등산에 관심을 갖게 하려고
⑤ 등산용품 세일에 대해 알려주려고

6 다음을 듣고, 남자가 가장 좋아하는 스포츠를 고르세요.

①  ②  ③  ④  ⑤ 

7 다음을 듣고, 아래 메뉴에서 <u>잘못된</u> 것을 고르세요.

Red Brick Cafe

Chef's Menu

① Fresh Caesar Salad
② French Onion Soup
③ Beef Roast with Vegetables
④ Cheese Plate
⑤ Chocolate Pastry

8 다음 광고를 듣고, 내용과 일치하지 <u>않는</u> 것을 고르세요.

① 여자의 취미는 분재 가꾸기이다.
② 분재는 가꾸기가 매우 쉽다.
③ 분재와 비디오를 함께 판매한다.
④ 비디오를 사면 사은품을 준다.
⑤ 수량이 충분하지 않으니 서둘러 주문해야 한다.

* Bonsai: 분재

1

M _________ _________ _________ _________ history, Kate?

W Yes, I am _________ _________ history. Why do you ask?

M The city is offering a tour of historic places.

W Oh, that _________ _________ fun!

M Yeah. They drive you around town and _________ _________.

W _________ _________! Would you like to go together?

M Yes, that would be great. _________ _________ _________ Saturday?

W You bet. I'll see you then.

2

W Are you going on the _________ _________ next week?

M I didn't know _________ _________ _________. Where is it?

W We are visiting a science lab _________ _________ _________.

M Oh, I _________ _________ _________ more about geology. But I might have plans already.

W Well, _________ _________, so you don't have to come.

M I really _________ _________, though. I'll look at my schedule.

W So will you _________ _________ _________?

3

M We should do something to _________ _________ _________.

W I agree. How about _________ _________ _________ in the park?

M That's a great idea. I have _________ _________ _________ helping the environment.

W Me too. Let's meet at the park tomorrow at 8:00.

M I'm going jogging at 8:00. How about meeting _________ _________ _________?

W My class starts _________ _________ _________. But it only lasts _________ _________.

M Then we'll meet when your class is _________.

4

M I have always had a _________ _________ cars. When I was a kid, I _________ _________ magazines about sports cars and the like. My father taught me _________ _________ _________ all kinds of car problems. By the time I was an adult, I knew all there was to know about _________ _________. It seemed natural that it would _________ _________ _________ one day. Now I get to do what I love _________ _________ _________.

5

W Hi, Jack. It's Marilyn.

M Hi, Marilyn. What's up?

W Well, you're _________ _________ mountain climbing, right?

M You know I _________ _________ mountains.

W I thought so. Are you aware of the _________ _________ at the sports equipment store?

M No, I didn't know there was a _________ _________ _________.

W Oh, you must go. They have _________ _________ on mountain climbing gear.

M That's great to hear. Thanks for _________ _________ _________.

6

M What do I enjoy in _________ _________ _________? Well, I do have a favorite sport. It isn't for everyone. You have to _________ _________ _________ it to really have a good time. Also, you have to _________ _________ _________ harsh conditions, like cold weather, snow, ice, and other things. But for me, there's _________ _________ _________ it. I love the feeling I get when I'm speeding down a mountain. I _________ _________ _________ every opportunity I get.

7

M Welcome to the Red Brick Cafe, where you'll find the best French food in the city. Are you _________ _________ the five-course chef's menu? It _________ _________ a fresh Caesar salad, followed by a hot bowl of rich French onion soup. We then serve the _________ _________, which is a beef roast with vegetables, followed by a plate of cheeses. Finally, for _________ we offer some delicious ice cream.

8

W Are you looking to _________ _________ a new hobby? Hobbies are a great way to _________ _________ _________ and add more fun to your life! My favorite hobby is _________ _________ my Bonsai tree. These beautiful plants can require _________ _________ _________ _________. But my new instructional video _________ _________ _________ for everyone! Order today to receive your own Bonsai and video, plus a _________ _________ from me! Supply is limited; this offer won't _________ _________!

WHERE CAN I FIND THE POST OFFICE?

소요 시간 묻고 답하기

~에 가는 데 얼마나 걸리니?	How long does/will it take to go to ~?
~ (정도) 걸려 / 걸릴 거야.	It takes (about) ~. / It'll take (about) ~.

거리 묻고 답하기

~에서 ~까지는 얼마나 머니?	How far is it from ~ to ~?
~ (정도) 거리야.	It's (about) ~.

위치 묻고 답하기

~이 어디에 있니?	Where can I find ~? / Where is ~?
(~에서) ~로 어떻게 가니?	How can/could/do I get to ~ (from ~)?
저쪽에 있어.	It's over there.
오른쪽/왼쪽으로 가. / 쭉 가.	Turn right/left. / Go straight.

Words   **_Getting Around_**

 destination    distance   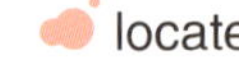 locate    mile    opposite    route

 schedule    track    transfer   vehicle   via   wander

01 대화를 듣고, 여자가 가고자 하는 기차역의 위치를 고르세요.

02 다음을 듣고, 내용과 일치하는 것을 모두 고르세요.

a The lecture will last 45 minutes.
b The students can study before the exam.
c A lecture will follow the exam.

03 주어진 표현을 사용하여 대화를 완성하세요.

How long does it take	Where can I find	It takes	turn left

A ___________________ track 7B? I seem to be lost.
B Go straight, then ___________________ at the newsstand.
A Great. ___________________ to get there? My train leaves in five minutes.
B ___________________ a minute or two. You'll be fine.

들려주는 내용을 잘 듣고 물음에 답하세요.

1 대화를 듣고, 남자가 이용할 교통수단을 고르세요.

① taxi　　② train　　③ bus　　④ subway　　⑤ walk

2 대화를 듣고, 남자가 가려고 하는 박물관의 위치를 고르세요.

3 다음 상황 설명을 듣고, Claire가 할 말로 가장 적절한 것을 고르세요.

Claire ____________________________________

① Can you please give me a ride?
② Where can I find my hotel?
③ I traveled to Paris last summer.
④ I need to report a crime.
⑤ What is the name of my hotel?

4 대화를 듣고, 상황을 가장 잘 나타낸 그림을 고르세요.

① ② ③ ④ ⑤

5 다음을 듣고, 아래 비행 일정표에서 <u>잘못된</u> 부분을 고르세요.

FLIGHTS

① Flight 1243

② **Departing**   4:40 / New York, NY / ③ Gate 23

④ **Arriving**   3:10 / ⑤ London, England

6 다음을 듣고, 남자가 하는 말의 목적으로 가장 적절한 것을 고르세요.

① 자신이 쓴 책을 광고하려고　　　　② 행복한 삶에 대해 조언하려고
③ 좋은 의사가 되는 방법을 알려주려고　　④ 자신의 경험을 이야기하려고
⑤ 좋은 책을 쓰는 비결을 알려주려고

7 대화를 듣고, 상황에 가장 잘 어울리는 속담을 고르세요.

① Make hay while the sun shines.　　② All's well that ends well.
③ The ends justify the means.　　④ Beggars can't be choosers.
⑤ Opportunity only knocks once.

8 대화를 듣고, 여자가 남자에게 부탁한 것을 고르세요.

① 해변까지 태워다 주기　　　　② 함께 여행 가기
③ 기차표를 예약하기　　　　④ 길을 알려주기
⑤ 기차 요금을 대신 내주기

1

M I'm new to the city. __________ __________ __________ __________ the post office?

W It's __________ __________ __________ from here.

M OK. What's __________ __________ __________ to get there?

W You could get a taxi, but traffic is terrible.

M True. __________ __________ the bus?

W It's cheap, but you'd __________ __________ __________ a couple of times.

M Hm. It's __________ __________ __________ __________. I guess the subway is the fastest route.

2

W Hey, Jim. Are you going somewhere?

M Yes, I'm meeting my friend at the museum. __________ __________ __________ __________ there?

W The __________ __________ is to go north on Fifth Street, past the park.

M OK. Is the museum on Fifth Street?

W No, you have to __________ __________ __________ Green Avenue. The museum is on __________ __________ __________ of the street from City Hall.

M OK. __________ __________ __________ __________ to the museum from the school?

W __________ __________ __________ __________. It's about three miles.

M Great! Thanks for your help, Jan.

3

W Last summer, Claire took a vacation to Paris. She didn't know the city, so she __________ __________ looking at the sights. One day, she wandered too far and found that __________ __________ __________. She needed to __________ __________ __________ her hotel but didn't know the way. She __________ the nearest policeman to see if he could help her. In this situation, what will Claire say?

4

M Hello, ma'am. Where can I take you?

W I need to __________ __________ for a meeting.

M Sure, I can take you there.

W __________ __________ __________ __________ __________ to get to the Harris Building?

M __________ __________ __________? Probably 20 minutes or more.

W But I thought it was just a couple of miles.

M It is. I only __________ __________ __________, though, so the fare will be cheap.

5

W Attention all passengers on flight _________. We are now boarding _________ _________ _________ at 4:40. Please report to _________ _________ to board your flight. That's flight 1243, nonstop to _________. It will take about five and a half hours to _________ _________ _________, where the local arrival time will be _________. Thank you.

6

M Hi. My name is Dr. James Wilson. A lot of people ask themselves, "_________ _________ _________ _________ happiness?" They _________ _________ happiness in jobs, in relationships, _________ _________ _________. But I'm here to tell you that it's right in front of you already. In my _________ _________ *The Secret to Happiness*, you'll _________ _________ _________ happiness in everyday things. So pick up a copy of my book today, and learn _________ _________ _________ _________ happiness.

7

M Hey, Julie. What's the matter?
W I wrecked my car today. Another _________ hit it on the freeway.
M Oh no! Well, I'm glad you aren't _________.
W Yeah, I guess so. Now I have to drive my parents' old car instead.
M _________ _________ you still have something to drive.
W I know, I know. But it's an old person's car! _________ _________!
M Just be _________ that you have a car at all.
W Yeah. I should _________ _________ _________, I guess.
M Sometimes you have to take _________ _________ _________ _________.

8

W Hey, Paul. _________ _________ does it take to go to Orange Beach?
M _________ _________ an hour or two, _________ _________ the type of transportation. Why?
W I thought you might want _________ _________ _________ at the coast this weekend.
M That sounds like fun. How do you want to _________ _________?
W Well, we could get there _________ _________. But there's a transfer.
M Oh, you're right. You can _________ _________ _________ _________ Central City.
W Still, it's probably _________ _________ _________. And cheaper.
M Great. I _________ _________ _________ it.

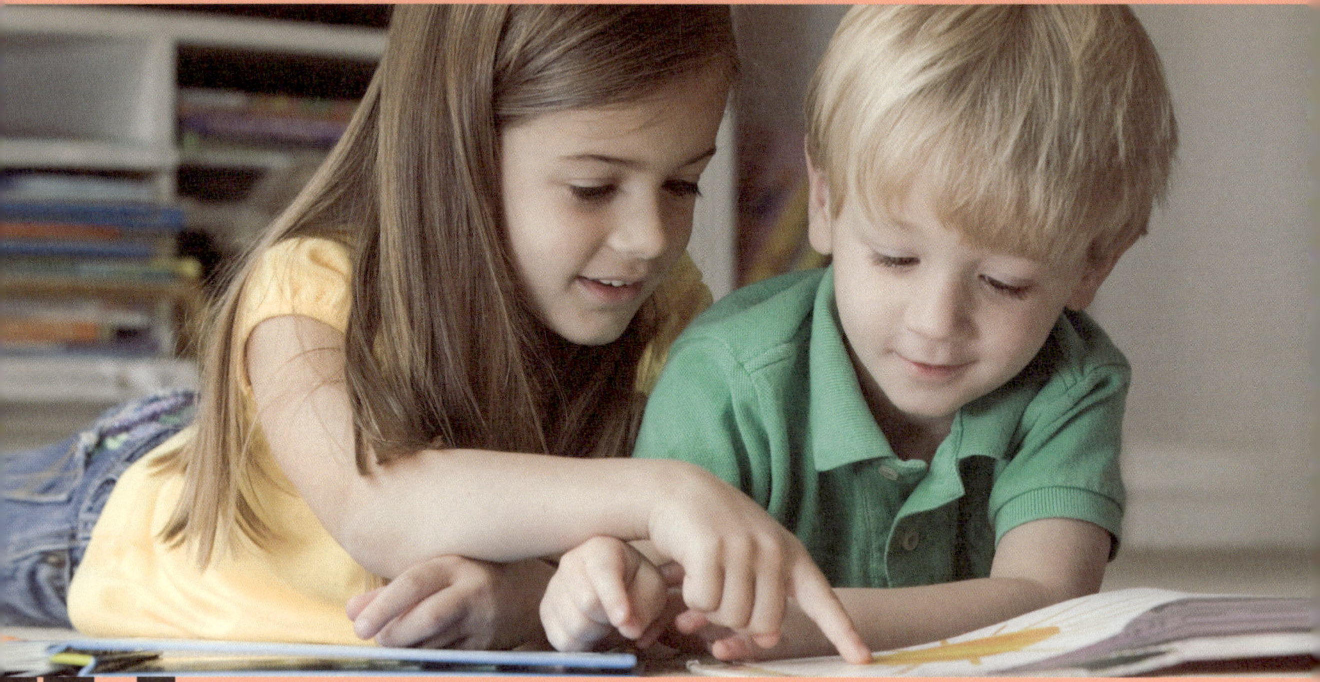

Ⅳ UNIT WHAT IS IT ABOUT?

사실적 정보 묻기

~은 무엇에 대한 거니?	What is ~ about?
너 왜 ~인지 아니?	Do you know why ~?
예전에는 어땠니?	What was it like before?
~에 대해 / ~을 말해줄래?	Can you tell me (about) ~?

답하기

응, 알아.	Yes, I know.
그것은 ~에 대한 거야.	It's about ~.
예전에는 ~했어.	It used to be ~.

보고하기

~이 …라고 말했어.	~ (has) told me/us (that) …
~이 …에 대해 말해줬어.	~ (has) told me/us about …

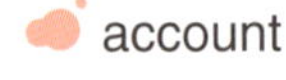 account  debt 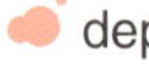 deposit  expense  fortune  invest

 loan  owe  salary  savings  sum   tax   tight

 **01** 다음 그림의 상황에 가장 잘 어울리는 대화를 고르세요.

02 대화를 듣고, 내용과 일치하면 T, 일치하지 않으면 F에 ✓ 표 하세요.

1 The man got a new haircut. T F
2 The woman noticed the haircut. T F
3 The woman doesn't like the haircut. T F

03 주어진 표현을 사용하여 대화를 완성하세요.

told me about that	Do you know why	Can you tell me	I know

A _________________ your parents named you John?

B _________________ that my grandfather's name is John. I think I'm named after him.

A Oh, that's right. I think you have _________________ before.

B _________________ where your name comes from?

들려주는 내용을 잘 듣고 물음에 답하세요.

1 대화를 듣고, 엄마가 아들에게 용돈을 주는 조건으로 부탁한 일을 고르세요.

① 집안일을 도울 것
② 비디오 게임을 하지 않을 것
③ 주말에 친구들을 만나지 말 것
④ 공부를 열심히 할 것
⑤ 나중에 돈을 갚을 것

2 대화를 듣고, 남자가 여자를 위해 하기로 한 것을 고르세요.

① 콘서트에 같기 가기
② CD를 함께 사기
③ CD 빌려주기
④ 돈 빌려주기
⑤ 은행에 같이 가주기

3 다음을 듣고, 아래 그래프에서 <u>잘못된</u> 것을 고르세요.

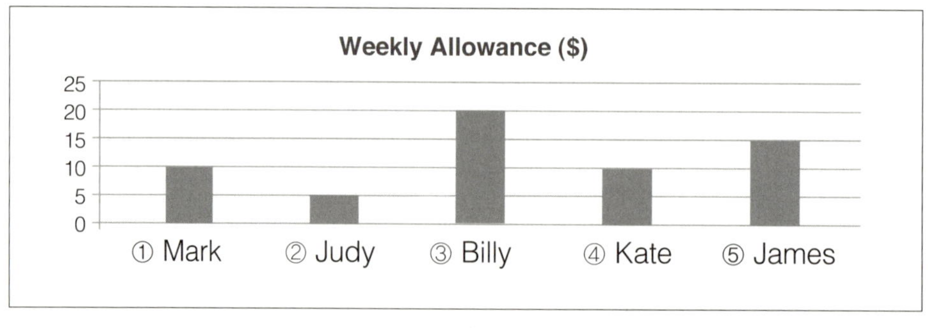

4 대화를 듣고, 두 사람이 무엇에 대해 이야기하고 있는지 고르세요.

① Being a lawyer
② How to make money
③ Jobs that pay a lot of money
④ A teacher's salary
⑤ Jobs they want to do

5 대화를 듣고, 남자의 문제가 무엇인지 고르세요.

① 버스를 탈 돈이 없다.
② 어떤 버스를 타야 할지 모른다.
③ 친구를 기다려야 한다.
④ 집에 가는 버스를 놓쳤다.
⑤ 버스 카드를 충전해야 한다.

6 다음을 듣고, 글의 종류로 가장 적절한 것을 고르세요.

① 신문 기사　　② 광고　　③ 편지　　④ 일기　　⑤ 소설

7 대화를 듣고, 대화가 이루어지는 장소로 가장 적절한 곳을 고르세요.

① a store
② a public library
③ a bank
④ a currency exchange
⑤ a courtroom

8 다음 짝지어진 대화 중 <u>어색한</u> 것을 고르세요.

①　　②　　③　　④　　⑤

다음을 듣고 빈칸에 들어갈 알맞은 말을 쓰세요.

1

M Hey, Mom? Can I have some __________ __________ __________ for the weekend?

W What do you need extra money for?

M __________ __________ __________, like a CD or a video game.

W You know I don't like you playing __________ __________ __________ __________.

M But I also have no money to __________ __________ __________ friends.

W OK, let's __________ __________ __________. If you help me __________ __________ __________, I'll give you a little more money.

M Thanks, Mom! __________ __________ __________!

2

W I want this CD __________ __________! It's my favorite band.

M Well, __________ __________ __________ buy it then?

W It's too expensive. I only have $5.

M __________ __________ __________ __________ __________ their music?

W Oh, it's the best. They play rock music.

M That __________ __________ __________ I would like, too.

W Do you want to __________ __________ __________?

M Sure, I have some money. We'll __________ it.

W That's very __________ of you!

3

M For my class project, I asked my friends about their __________ __________. Then I made this chart to show __________ __________ __________ they get each week. My friend Mark told me that he gets $__________ a week from his parents. Judy, however, only gets __________ __________ __________ __________ __________ Mark. Billy and Kate get the __________ __________ __________ at $__________ per week. And James receives $ __________ a week from his grandmother.

4

W What do you want to be __________ __________ __________ __________, Michael?

M I want to be a __________. They make a really high __________.

W You mean they make a lot of money?

M Yeah, that's what salary is. It's __________ __________ __________ __________ __________.

W Well, I want to be a __________ when I grow up.

M Really? __________ __________?

W I like teaching people things. __________ __________ __________ a lot of money though.

M Yes, I know. Then why would you want to do it?

W __________ __________ __________ __________. To me, that's more important than money.

5

W _________ _________, Ken! You'll miss the bus!

M _________ _________, but I have a small problem.

W _________ _________ _________? Maybe I can help.

M I can't find my _________ _________. And I didn't bring any money.

W Uh-oh. They won't _________ _________ _________ the bus then.

M I know. Do you have any _________ _________?

W I can _________ _________ a dollar, if you want.

M That'd be great. I'll _________ _________ _________ tomorrow.

6

M Do you want to be rich? _________ _________ _________! Everyone wants to have _________ _________. Well, today I'm going to tell you the _________ _________ getting rich fast. It's all in my _________ _________, called *More Money Now*! Do you know _________ _________ _________ to be successful? Do you want to know the secrets of rich people? For the _________ _________ of $35, you get the answers to these questions and more. So call today and _________ _________ _________!

7

W Good morning. How can I help you?

M I'd like to _________ _________ _________, please.

W I'd be happy to help. Will that be checking or savings?

M I want to open a _________ _________.

W I just need you to _________ _________ this paperwork.

M Of course. And I brought some money for _________ _________ _________.

W Great. We'll have your account _________ _________ in just a moment.

8

① M _________ _________ _________ this is the correct building?

W It is the address _________ _________ _________.

② M I think we should _________ _________ the stock market.

W Sure, I'll go to the market with you.

③ M _________ _________ _________ _________ the dinosaurs died?

W I hear there are _________ _________ _________ _________, but no one really knows.

④ M My teacher _________ _________ _________ that I should talk more in class.

W I agree. You have some very smart things to say.

⑤ M _________ _________ _________ be easy to get good grades.

W I know. High school is _________ _________ _________!

UNIT V DO YOU MIND IF WE TALK ABOUT IT?

허락 요청하기

~해도 괜찮겠니?	Do you mind if ~? / Is OK if ~?
내가 ~해도 되니?	May/Can I ~?
~하게 해줘.	Let me ~.

허락하기

그럼. / 괜찮아.	Sure. / Of course. / OK. / Go ahead.
마음대로 ~해.	Feel free to ~.
난 괜찮아.	Not at all. / Of course not. (Do you mind ~?에 대한 대답)

허락하지 않기

미안하지만 안 되겠어.	I'm afraid not. / (I'm) Sorry, but ~.
그러고 싶지만 ~.	I'd like ~ but ~.
절대 안 돼.	No way.

Words   *Feelings*

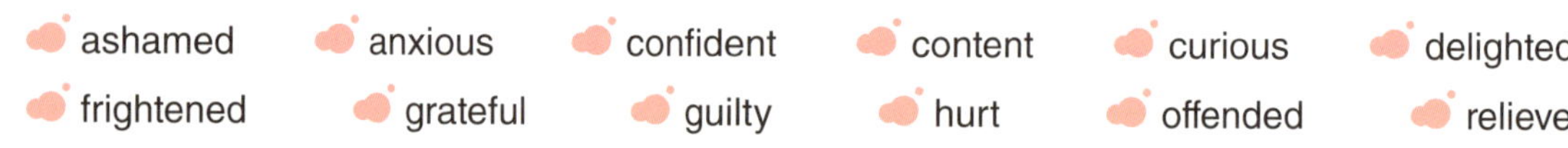

ashamed   anxious   confident   content   curious   delighted

frightened   grateful   guilty   hurt   offended   relieved

 **01** 대화를 듣고, 남자의 심정을 가장 잘 나타낸 그림을 고르세요.

 **02** 대화를 듣고, 내용과 일치하는 것을 모두 고르세요.

a The woman is traveling for the holidays.
b The woman has work to do at home.
c The man is curious about the woman's plans.

03 주어진 표현을 사용하여 대화를 완성하세요.

Do you mind if	Not at all	Is it OK if	I'm afraid not

A _________________ I borrow your textbook today?
B _________________ . I need it to read during class.
A OK. _________________ I read along with you then?
B _________________ . That'd be fine.

들려주는 내용을 잘 듣고 물음에 답하세요.

1 대화를 듣고, 대화의 내용과 일치하지 <u>않는</u> 것을 고르세요.

① 여자는 금요일에 시험이 있다.
② 여자는 초조해하고 있다.
③ 여자는 수업시간에 잘 집중하지 않는다.
④ 남자는 수업시간에 필기를 잘 한다.
⑤ 남자는 여자에게 필기한 것을 빌려주기로 했다.

2 다음 상황 설명을 듣고, Greg가 뒤에 앉은 사람들에게 할 말로 가장 적절한 것을 고르세요.

Greg ____________________________

① I'd like to move seats.
② Do you mind being a little quieter?
③ We will be leaving now.
④ What are you talking about?
⑤ How are you doing today?

3 다음을 듣고, 여자의 직업을 고르세요.

① banker　　　② secretary　　　③ nurse
④ saleswoman　　　⑤ store manager

4 대화를 듣고, 현재 예상되는 비행기의 도착 시간을 고르세요.

① 4:00　　　② 4:30　　　③ 5:00
④ 5:30　　　⑤ 6:00

5 대화를 듣고, 남자가 사려는 것을 고르세요.

① 보석　　　　② 상품권　　　　③ 드레스　　　　④ 장갑　　　　⑤ 스카프

6 그림과 그에 대한 설명이 일치하지 <u>않는</u> 것을 고르세요.

①　　　　②　　　　③　　　　④　　　　⑤

7 다음을 듣고, 남자가 마지막에 느꼈을 심정으로 가장 적절한 것을 고르세요.

① nervous　　　　② frightened　　　　③ relieved
④ excited　　　　⑤ surprised

8 대화를 듣고, 아래 초대장에서 <u>잘못된</u> 부분을 고르세요.

You're Invited!

① What: Jen's birthday party
② Where: Jack's house
③ When: Tuesday night
④ We will have pizza and games!
⑤ Please RSVP by Sunday!

* RSVP: 초대에 대한 회신을 달라는 뜻

다음을 듣고 빈칸에 들어갈 알맞은 말을 쓰세요.

1

M What's the matter, Pam?
W I have a test on Friday, and I feel __________ __________ __________.
M Why so nervous? I'm sure __________ __________ __________.
W I haven't been listening much in class.
M __________ __________ __________.
W No, and my notes aren't so great either.
M I always __________ really careful __________.
W __________ __________ __________ __________ I borrow them, to study?
M I __________ __________ that would be right.

2

M Greg was at a movie __________ __________ __________. He was having a lot of fun, until some people behind him started __________ __________ during the film. He didn't want to move seats, but he __________ __________ __________ all of their rude behavior. Greg __________ __________ to face the loud people. In this situation, what would Greg say?

3

W My job requires me to be very __________. I have to talk to new people all the time, and I need them to __________ __________. It is my job to make them believe that they __________ __________ __________ what I have. If they don't trust me, then they likely won't want to __________ __________ __________ __________. All in all, I'm pretty good at my job, and it still feels great to __________ __________ __________.

4

M Excuse me, ma'am? __________ __________ __________ you a question?
W __________ __________. What is it?
M When will flight 113 arrive?
W Oh yes. The flight was __________ __________ __________. It was supposed to arrive at 4:00. It was an hour late leaving Los Angeles.
M OK. Are there any other problems?
W Also, because of the storms, the plane could take an __________ __________ __________ to land.
M Thank you, I'm very __________ for your help.
W It's no trouble, sir.

5

M I'm looking for a present for my niece.
W Oh? __________ __________ __________?

M Last week was her birthday. _________ _________ _________ for missing it.

W Well, we have a great _________ _________ _________.

M I don't have much money, actually.

W How about _________ _________ _________?

M I'm afraid I don't know her size.

W You could always buy her a _________ _________.

M I want to get something _________ _________.

W Over here, we have _________ _________ _________ of winter scarves and gloves.

M Oh, those look nice. I think she'll be content with a _________ _________.

W OK. Can I _________ _________ _________ for you?

6

M ① The boy is playing _________ with his dog.

② The children are building a _________ _________.

③ The girl is _________ of the mouse.

④ The boy is playing an _________ _________.

⑤ The kids are eating _________ _________ together.

7

M The alarm clock _________ _________, and I sat up in bed. I looked at the clock. It was already 7:30, and I had to _________ _________ _________ at 8:00. I _________!
I couldn't be late for class again. I'd be _________ _________! So I took the fastest shower that I could, threw on _________ _________, grabbed my bag, and ran for _________ _________ _________. Just as I arrived, the bus was _________ _________.
I yelled, "Please, let me on the bus!" And surprisingly, it stopped. I got on it and sat down. My _________ _________ _________.

8

M Are you going to Jen's birthday party?

W Of course! It would _________ _________ _________ if I didn't.

M Yeah, that's true. Can I _________ _________ _________ Jack's house?

W Sure, I'll email them to you. You know the party is _________, right?

M Yeah, I read that on the invitation. Do you know if there will be food?

W Yes. The plan is to _________ _________ and play games.

M That sounds like fun. _________ _________ _________ Jen tonight and tell her I'm attending.

W Please do. They asked everyone to RSVP _________ _________.

VI DO YOU REMEMBER?

기억 묻기

너 ~ 기억하니?	(Do you) Remember ~?
너 ~ 잊어버렸니?	Have you forgotten ~?

답하기(긍정)

(물론) 기억해.	(Yes/Sure/Of course), I remember.
난 ~을 절대 잊지 않을 거야.	I'll never forget ~.
난 생생히 기억해.	I remember it well/clearly.

답하기(부정)

그 일에 대해 잊어버렸어.	I forgot about that.
~이 기억이 안 나.	I can't remember ~.
깜빡 잊어버렸네.	It slipped my mind.
잠깐만. 기억하려고 노력 중이야.	Wait a minute. I'm trying to remember.

Words   **Life**

 achieve    after all   attempt   challenge   childhood   effort

in the end   in those days   memory   past   once in a while

01 그림에 나타난 상황을 가장 잘 설명하는 문장을 고르세요.

02 대화를 듣고, 내용과 일치하면 T, 일치하지 않으면 F에 ✓ 표 하세요.

1 The speakers took a vacation to the beach. T F
2 The man saw the ocean for the first time. T F
3 Neither speaker really wants to go back. T F

03 주어진 표현을 사용하여 대화를 완성하세요.

slipped my mind	have you forgotten	I can't remember

A John, __________________ your lunch again?
B __________________ if I brought it to school or not.
A Maybe you left it at your house.
B Probably so. It must have __________________.

들려주는 내용을 잘 듣고 물음에 답하세요.

1 대화를 듣고, 두 사람이 무엇에 대해 이야기하고 있는지 고르세요.

① 첫 번째 데이트   ② 학교 친구들   ③ 새로 산 코트
④ 여자의 비상한 기억력   ⑤ 등교 첫 날

2 대화를 듣고, 여자의 마지막 말에 대해 남자가 할 말로 가장 적절한 것을 고르세요.

M	

① No, I want to be a teenager again.
② Yes, my life is much better in the present.
③ Maybe, but being a teen was fun.
④ No, I don't think you would like it.
⑤ Yes, being a teenager was easy for you.

3 다음을 듣고, 여자가 편지를 쓴 목적을 고르세요.

① to complain   ② to compliment   ③ to remind
④ to congratulate   ⑤ to apologize

4 대화를 듣고, 체육관의 위치를 고르세요.

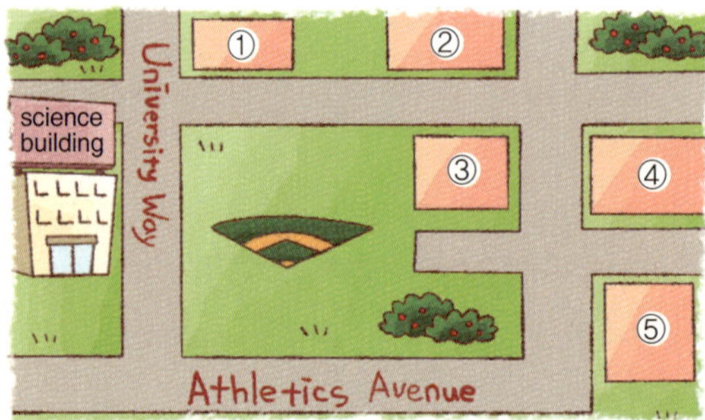

5 대화를 듣고, 두 사람이 본 영화에 대한 설명으로 <u>잘못된</u> 것을 고르세요

① 지난주에 보았다.　　　　　　　　② 서부 영화였다.

③ 주인공은 악당들에 맞서 싸웠다.　　④ 남자는 액션 장면을 좋아했다.

⑤ 마지막에 주인공이 죽었다.

6 다음을 듣고, 아래 포스터에서 <u>잘못된</u> 것을 고르세요.

7 대화를 듣고, 두 사람의 관계로 가장 적절한 것을 고르세요.

① mother – son　　　　　　　② father – daughter

③ boyfriend – girlfriend　　　　④ clerk – customer

⑤ sister – brother

8 다음을 듣고, 언급되지 <u>않은</u> 것을 고르세요.

① 아빠가 야구 배트를 사주신 것　　② 핫도그를 먹은 것　　③ 팝콘을 먹은 것

④ 야구선수들의 사인을 받은 것　　⑤ 관중들의 함성을 들은 것

다음을 듣고 빈칸에 들어갈 알맞은 말을 쓰세요.

1

M __________ __________ __________ your first day of school?

W Of course. I remember. I was __________ __________!

M Me too. __________ __________, it was such a new experience.

W I __________ __________ you forgot your coat, so I lent you mine.

M I __________ __________ __________. What a great memory!

W Yes. That was when we first became friends.

2

W __________ __________ __________ what it was like to be a teenager?

M Yeah. I don't want to __________ __________ that again.

W Whatever do you mean?

M I got __________ __________ a lot in those days.

W You mean, by __________?

M Yeah, they made fun of me __________ __________ __________.

W I'm sorry to hear that. Aren't you glad it's __________ __________ __________?

3

W Dear Parents,

I hope this letter finds you and your children well. I thank you __________ __________ the school meeting last Friday afternoon. I just wanted to __________ __________ __________ the big event that is coming next week. __________ __________ __________? It's the Spring Festival, and everyone is invited! We are also __________ __________ volunteers to sell food and work __________ __________ __________. Please let me know if you are interested in __________ __________ __________.

Sincerely,
Principal Victoria

4

W Hey, Jack. __________ __________ __________ __________ our workout?

M You know I forget things __________ __________ __________ __________. Where is the gym again?

W Start at the science building and __________ __________ __________ University Way.

M OK. And what then?

W Take the __________ __________ and drive past the baseball fields.

M And then?

W Turn left again at the next intersection. The gym will be the ________ ________ ________ ________ ________.

M Thanks, I'll be there in a minute.

5

M What was the ________ ________ ________ ________ we saw last week?

W ________ ________ ________ ________? It was called *Law Man*.

M Oh, right. Now ________ ________. It was a Western, right?

W Yeah. It was about a man's attempt to save his town from outlaws.

M Of course! ________ ________ ________ were really amazing.

W Yes, but ________ ________ ________, the cowboy defeated the bad guys and saved the day.

6

M Do you know what time it is? ________ ________ ________ ________ for the citywide hot dog eating contest, held every year! Last year's winner ate ________ ________ hot dogs! If you think you can ________ ________ ________, call us today at 555-________ to enter the contest. The event begins at ________ in the City High School gym, but all eaters in the contest should ________ ________ an hour early.

7

W I remember when I was ________ ________, Danny.

M Really? What was ________ ________ ________?

W Well, 30 years ago, we didn't have any of ________ ________ ________ that you have now.

M What did you ________ ________ ________?

W We played outside all day, and we ________ ________ ________ ________ at night.

M You didn't have TV ________ ________?

W Oh no, it was still new then, and much too expensive.

8

M ________ ________ ________ the first time my dad took me to a baseball game. I was ________ ________. I can still hear the ________ ________. I can still smell the popcorn and the hot dogs. My dad bought me a new ________ ________ just for that game. After the game, we even got the players' autographs. It was ________ ________ ________ of my life.

VII ARE YOU SURE?

확신 여부 묻기

너 (그것에 대해) 확신해?	Are you sure (about that)?
너 진심이야?	Are you serious?

답하기(긍정)

(~인 것이) 확실해.	I'm sure/confident (that ~).
정말 확실해.	I'm pretty/absolutely sure.
정말이야. / 농담 아니야.	I mean it. / I'm serious. / I'm not joking.

답하기(부정)

잘 모르겠어. (하지만 ~)	I'm not sure, (but ~).
(~에 대해) 확실치 않아.	I'm not certain (about ~).
(~인지) 잘 모르겠어.	I don't know (if ~).

Words · *Time*

- as soon as
- at the moment
- at the same time
- delay
- exact/exactly
- extension
- interval
- period
- urgent

 대화를 듣고, 상황을 가장 잘 나타낸 그림을 고르세요.

 대화를 듣고, 해당하는 것에 ✓ 표 하세요.

	Frogs	Toads
Have rough, dry skin		
Always live near water		
Have wet, smooth skin		

03 주어진 표현을 사용하여 대화를 완성하세요.

I'm confident	Are you sure	I'm not sure

A Did you know dogs and cats have feelings, just like people?

B ___________________ about that? I've always been told that they don't.

A ___________________ of it. My cat shows her feelings all the time.

B ___________________, but I think they feel things differently than people.

들려주는 내용을 잘 듣고 물음에 답하세요.

1 대화를 듣고, 대화가 이루어지는 장소로 가장 적절한 곳을 고르세요.

① 서점　　　　　② 슈퍼마켓　　　　　③ 컴퓨터실
④ 호텔　　　　　⑤ 도서관

2 다음을 듣고, 글의 종류로 가장 적절한 것을 고르세요.

① letter　　　　　② speech　　　　　③ announcement
④ invitation　　　　　⑤ news story

3 대화를 듣고, 여자가 언제까지 과제를 제출해야 하는지 고르세요.

① Friday　　　　　② Saturday　　　　　③ Monday
④ Thursday　　　　　⑤ Wednesday

4 대화를 듣고, 여자가 목걸이를 놓아둔 곳을 고르세요.

① 　② 　③ 　④ 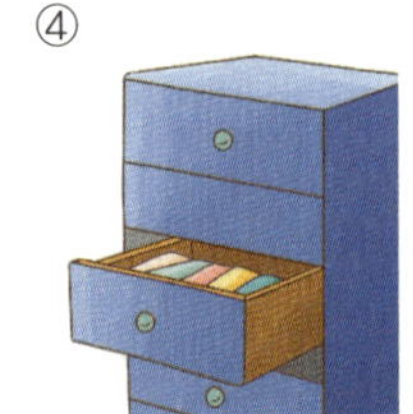　⑤ 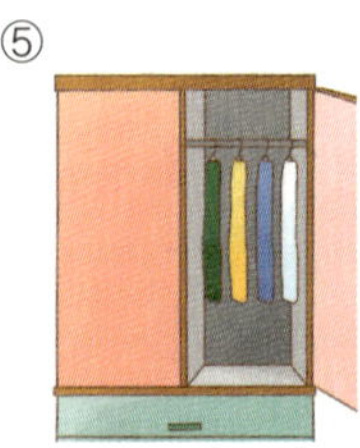

5 다음을 듣고, 내용과 일치하지 <u>않는</u> 것을 고르세요.

① People should not get too close to the cages.
② The gorillas are on display for a short time.
③ A new animal exhibit is on display.
④ People should hurry to see the gorillas.
⑤ The gorilla exhibit is now closed.

6 대화를 듣고, 아래 강의 시간표에서 <u>잘못된</u> 것을 고르세요.

	Monday	Tuesday	Wednesday	Thursday	Friday
6:00	① Spanish				⑤ German
7:00		② French	③ Japanese		
8:00				④ English	

7 다음 상황 설명을 듣고, Mary가 호스텔 직원에게 할 말로 가장 적절한 것을 고르세요.

Mary

① Can you direct me to a hotel?
② Where is your bathroom?
③ Do you speak English?
④ Can I rent a room for the night?
⑤ Where can I find a restaurant?

8 다음 중 <u>어색한</u> 대화를 고르세요.

①　　　　②　　　　③　　　　④　　　　⑤

다음을 듣고 빈칸에 들어갈 알맞은 말을 쓰세요.

1

W Are you ready to ________ ________, sir?
M Yes, ma'am. I have ________ ________ here.
W OK. Just ________ ________ ________ them into the computer.
M When ________ ________ ________ them?
W They are ________ ________ in exactly two weeks.
M Thanks, I'll probably ________ ________ a little early.

2

M ________, all passengers. We ________ ________ ________ you that there is still some ice on the runway. The crew is working hard to clear it up. ________ ________ ________ when we'll be able to take off, but I'm ________ ________ it will be soon. Until then, we will be experiencing a slight ________. We thank you for your patience.

3

W Hi, Mr. Robinson. I need to speak with you about my essay.
M Sure. What ________ ________ ________ the problem?
W Well, I'm going on vacation this week.
M You know the essay is ________ ________ ________, right?
W I know. But since I'll be out of town…
M You ________ ________ ________ on the deadline.
W If you're willing to give me one, yes.
M I'll let you turn it in ________ ________ ________ the deadline. But no later.
W ________ ________ ________ I can do that. Thanks!

4

M ________ ________ ________ to go to the party?
W Not yet. I can't find my necklace.
M ________ ________ ________? We're already late.
W ________ ________ ________ I find it, we'll go.
M Where do you think it might be?
W Well, I picked it up off the ________ ________.
M OK. Is it on the bed next to the table?
W No, I looked there already. After the bed, I went ________ ________ ________ to get a sweater.
M What about when you were ________ ________ ________?
W No, I didn't take it off then.
M I also saw you over ________ ________ ________.
W That must be where I left it!

5

W Thank you for visiting City Zoo. We hope you enjoy __________ __________. We'd like to remind you __________ __________ __________ the cages too closely. This may __________ __________ __________. Also, we'd like to remind you of our __________ __________. For a short period, we have two new gorillas __________ __________. Hurry and see them now, because they won't be here __________ __________. We're __________ you'll love it!

6

M Did you __________ __________ the foreign language classes?

W Yeah, the community college __________ __________ at night.

M Do you know the __________ __________ __________ of the classes?

W Well, there's __________ at 6:00 on __________.

M What about French?

W __________ __________ is at 7:00 on Tuesday.

M Are you __________ __________ __________? I heard French is on Wednesday.

W No, Wednesday is __________ at __________.

M Oh, you're right. Do you think you'll __________ __________ __________?

W I'm not sure __________ __________ __________. Either English, at 8:00 on Thursdays, or German, at 6:00 on Fridays.

7

W Mary arrives in Spain __________ __________. She is so excited to finally be there! Unfortunately, she didn't __________ __________ __________ with her, and now she needs a __________ __________ __________ for the night. It is getting dark, so the situation is __________. She finds a small hostel and walks __________ __________ __________ __________. She pulls all the money __________ __________ __________ __________ and shows it to the desk clerk. In this situation, what is Mary __________ __________ __________?

8

① **M** Would you like to __________ __________ __________ __________ with me?

   W I wish I could, but I'm very busy __________ __________ __________.

② **M** Do you think you passed __________ __________ __________?

   W No, I think I left my homework __________ __________ __________.

③ **M** When does the __________ __________ __________?

   W The buses come in 10-minute __________.

④ **M** Let's see if __________ __________ on TV.

   W Are you serious? __________ __________ __________ be studying.

⑤ **M** __________ __________ __________ that Matt will meet us there?

   W Yes, he __________ __________ meet him at the restaurant.

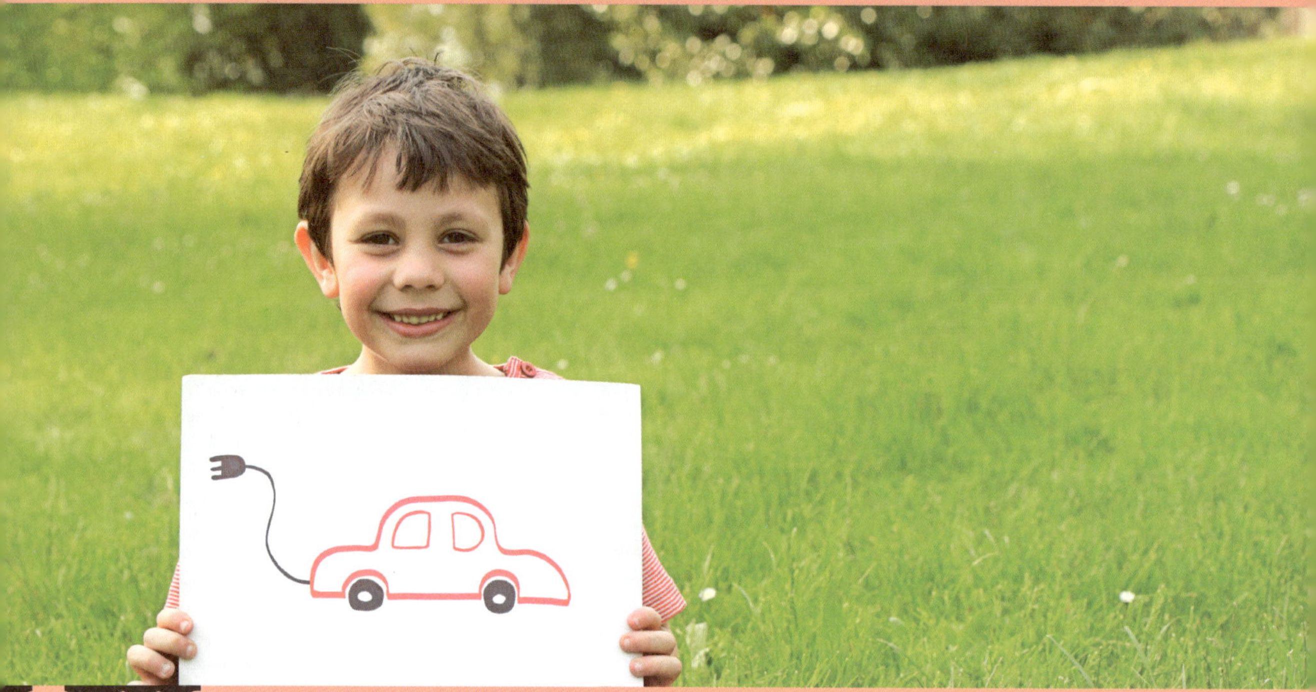

VIII GUESS WHAT!

추측하기

~일 것 같아.	I guess ~.
~인 것이 틀림없어.	~ must be ~.
~인 것이 분명해.	I bet ~.
내가 짐작하기로는 ~일 거야.	My guess is ~.

주의 끌기

잠시 안내 말씀 드립니다.	May I have your attention, (please)?
있잖아.	You know what?
(무슨 일인지) 맞춰 봐!	Guess what!
여기 봐. / 들어 봐.	Look. / Listen.
실례합니다.	Excuse me.

Words — Change

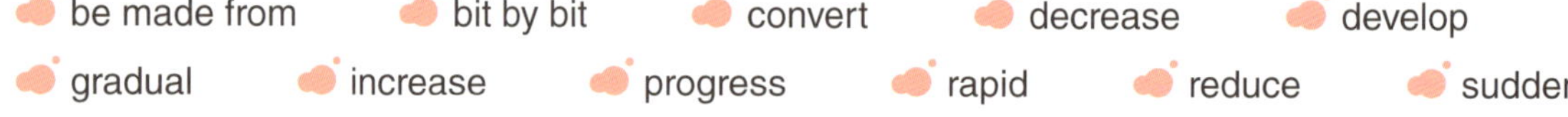

 다음 그림의 상황에 가장 잘 어울리는 대화를 고르세요.

 다음을 듣고, 내용과 일치하는 것을 고르세요.

a The woman is a professional chef.
b The woman used too much flour.
c The cake turned out quite well.

03 주어진 표현을 사용하여 대화를 완성하세요.

Guess what	I bet	He must be	My guess is

A ____________________ happened to Carl today at school?
B I heard he got into a fight. ____________________ in big trouble now.
A You got that right. ____________________ he'll be kicked out of school.
B ____________________ you're right. Poor Carl!

들려주는 내용을 잘 듣고 물음에 답하세요.

1 대화를 듣고, 두 사람의 관계로 가장 적절한 것을 고르세요.

  ① 교사와 학생 ② 엄마와 아들 ③ 동료 교사 ④ 학교 친구 ⑤ 이모와 조카

2 그림에 대한 설명이 그림과 일치하지 <u>않는</u> 것을 고르세요.

①    ②    ③    ④    ⑤ 

3 대화를 듣고, 여자가 지불할 금액을 고르세요.

LUNCH MENU

Chef's Salad	$4
Caesar Salad	$3
Vegetable Soup	$5
Clam Chowder	$4
Club Sandwich	$7
Chicken Sandwich	$6

  ① $4 ② $7 ③ $9 ④ $12 ⑤ $16

4 다음을 듣고, 마지막에 들려주는 질문에 대한 답을 고르세요.

  ① 주례가 주례사를 하고 있다. ② 신랑의 아버지가 하객들에게 인사를 하고 있다.
  ③ 신부의 아버지가 결혼식 축사를 하고 있다. ④ 사회자가 결혼식 일정을 안내하고 있다.
  ⑤ 신랑이 하객들에게 건배를 청하고 있다.

---

5 대화를 듣고, 여자가 남자에게 조언한 것을 고르세요.

① planting a new garden
② increasing the sunlight
③ watering the plants less
④ being less patient
⑤ planting more plants

---

6 다음 강의를 듣고, 강의의 주제를 고르세요.

① 광합성의 원리
② 인체의 신비
③ 자동차의 작동 원리
④ 비타민의 종류
⑤ 영양 섭취의 중요성

---

7 대화를 듣고, 아래 메모에서 <u>잘못된</u> 부분을 고르세요.

MISSED CALL

① To: Mike
② From: Carol
③ What: Meet up later
④ Where: At the mall
⑤ When: After school

---

8 다음을 듣고, 남자의 직업을 고르세요.

① doctor
② scientist
③ nurse
④ engineer
⑤ professor

다음을 듣고 빈칸에 들어갈 알맞은 말을 쓰세요.

1

W How is your __________ __________ going?

M I'm making a lot of progress. __________ __________, I'm almost finished.

W __________ __________ __________ working really hard then.

M Oh, I am. I'm up late every night __________ __________ it.

W Well, I hope you get __________ __________ __________ for your work.

M Thanks, and __________ __________ __________ your project as well.

2

M ① The girl is trying to __________ __________ __________.

② The boy is __________ __________ __________ in a bowl.

③ The boy is sleeping at his __________ __________.

④ The girl is __________ in the park.

⑤ The girl is __________ __________ __________ to school.

3

M Do you know what you'd __________ __________ __________, ma'am?

W Yes, I'll have the chef's salad __________ __________.

M Excellent choice. And __________ __________?

W Also, a bowl of vegetable soup. Is it made __________ __________ __________?

M Only the freshest, ma'am. __________ __________ __________ __________?

W __________ __________ __________? I'll have a club sandwich, too.

M OK. Your food should be ready shortly.

4

M May I __________ __________ __________, please? Thank you all for coming to my __________ __________. It truly has been a wonderful day. It seems like just yesterday, my daughter was a little girl. And __________, she has become an adult. But I'm __________ __________ she and her new husband will be happy for __________ __________ __________ __________.

Dictation

5

M I'm _________ _________ my garden. I planted it weeks ago, but nothing is growing.

W These things _________ _________. Plants grow _________ _________.

M You're right. I guess I'm just _________ _________.

W Probably so. Are you watering them _________?

M Yes. But they don't get _________ _________ sunlight as they could.

W _________ _________ _________ the amount of sun, and see _________ _________.

M OK. Thanks for the help, Pam.

6

M OK, class, please _________ _________. Today in health class we will be _________
_________ _________. Basically, your body uses food like a car _________ _________.
It takes all the vitamins and minerals _________ _________ _________ and rapidly
converts them into energy. Without these things, your body would quickly _________
_________, just like a car that is _________ _________ _________. This is why you can
_________ _________ _________. As you decrease your food, your body produces less
and _________ _________.

7

M Hello?

W Hi, this is Carol. I'm _________ _________ Mike.

M Oh, I'm afraid Mike is out right now. Shall I take a message?

W Can you tell Mike _________ _________ _________ after school?

M Sure. Where should he meet you?

W _________ _________ _________. We planned to study together today.

M OK. I'll _________ _________ _________.

W Thanks, Mr. Weathers!

8

M _________ _________ _________? I couldn't ask for a better job. Every day, my
coworkers and I work hard to _________ _________ _________. Our goal is to make life
easier for people. We work to reduce the amount of _________ and _________ in the
world. In that way, I always feel like I'm _________ _________ _________ to make the
world a better place.

IX YOU'RE SUPPOSED TO BE CAREFUL.

의무 표현하기

넌 ~하기로 되어 있어[~해야 해].	You're supposed to ~.
넌 반드시 ~해야 해.	You must ~.
넌 ~해야 해.	You have to ~.

경고하기

반드시 ~하도록 해.	Make sure ~.
~을 할 준비를 해.	Be ready for ~.
~을 하도록 / ~하지 않도록 주의해.	Be careful (not) to ~.
조심해!	(Be) Careful! / Watch out! / Look out!
~을 주의해.	Be careful with ~. / Watch out for ~.

Words　*Cooking*

- barbecue
- blend
- broil
- chop
- measure
- mix
- oven/stove
- overcook
- pour
- roast
- seasoning
- serve
- steam
- stir

54

01 

대화를 듣고, 두 사람이 이야기하고 있는 표지판을 고르세요.

a   b   c

02 

대화를 듣고, 내용과 일치하면 T, 일치하지 않으면 F에 ✓ 표 하세요.

1 남자는 유명한 요리사이다.   T F

2 여자는 남자의 요리를 좋아한다.   T F

3 남자는 여자에게 비결을 알려주지 않았다.   T F

03 주어진 표현을 사용하여 대화를 완성하세요.

I have to	make sure	be careful	you're supposed to

A Grace, _________________ be doing your homework.

B Do _______________? I'd rather be watching television.

A Right now, _________________ you finish that homework assignment.
And _________________ not to make any mistakes.

B OK, Dad. I will.

들려주는 내용을 잘 듣고 물음에 답하세요.

1 대화를 듣고, 여자가 종업원을 부른 이유가 무엇인지 고르세요.

① 요리가 차게 식어서
② 계산서를 요청하려고
③ 스테이크 요리가 잘못돼서
④ 여자가 주문한 요리가 나오지 않아서
⑤ 다른 요리를 추가로 주문하려고

2 대화를 듣고, 여자의 마지막 말에 대한 남자의 응답으로 가장 적절한 것을 고르세요.

M

① Yes, I like vegetables a lot.
② I'm not sure how to do that.
③ No, thanks. I know all about it.
④ Yes, please chop more vegetables.
⑤ We'll see about it later.

3 다음을 듣고, 어디에서 들을 수 있는 내용인지 고르세요.

① 강연회
② 요리 교실
③ 음식점
④ 호텔 뷔페
⑤ 마트의 시식 코너

4 대화를 듣고, 마지막에 들려주는 질문에 대한 답을 고르세요.

① Talking to her old friends
② Cooking for her parents
③ Taking a vacation
④ Her mother's cooking
⑤ Her parent's house

5 대화를 듣고, 대화를 통해 알 수 <u>없는</u> 것을 고르세요.

① 남자의 생일이 다가오고 있다.
② 여자는 남자를 위해 요리를 할 것이다.
③ 남자는 친구들을 생일 파티에 초대할 것이다.
④ 남자는 바닷가재 요리를 좋아한다.
⑤ 여자는 바닷가재 요리법을 정확히 모르고 있다.

* lobster: 바닷가재

6 다음을 듣고, 무엇에 관한 내용인지 고르세요.

① How to make barbecue　　② The importance of barbecue
③ The history of barbecue　　④ Cooking tough meat
⑤ Meats used in barbecue

7 다음을 듣고, 남자의 취미를 고르세요.

① 그림 그리기　　② 집 수리하기　　③ 목공 일 하기
④ 가구 수집하기　　⑤ 조각하기

8 대화를 듣고, 두 사람이 이야기하고 있는 그림을 고르세요.

①　　②　　③　　④　　⑤

다음을 듣고 빈칸에 들어갈 알맞은 말을 쓰세요.

1

W ___________ ___________, waiter?

M How can I help you, ma'am?

W I'm afraid ___________ ___________ ___________ ___________ with my food.

M Oh, I'm very sorry to hear that. What seems to be ___________ ___________?

W Well, my steak is ___________. It's very ___________ ___________ ___________.

M I'd be happy to have the chef cook you another.

W That's fine. Just ___________ ___________ ___________ ___________ overcook it again.

2

W Mike, will you help me in the kitchen?

M Sure, I'm ___________ ___________ in the kitchen. What would you like me to do?

W ___________ some fresh vegetables for dinner, please.

M ___________ ___________. Would you like me to cook them?

W Yes, if ___________ ___________ ___________. I was going to steam them.

M Oh, I love steamed vegetables. I make them at home ___________ ___________ ___________.

W Great. Do you think you'll ___________ ___________ ___________?

3

W OK, everyone. First we're going to ___________ ___________ ___________, flour, and eggs in one bowl. Stir that mixture until it all ___________ ___________. When it thickens, it's ready to go into the cake pan. ___________ ___________ ___________ into the pan and set the oven for 350 degrees. ___________ for about 30 minutes. You have to check it ___________ ___________ ___________, to make sure it's cooking properly, so ___________ ___________ ___________.

4

M What are you doing this weekend, Bernice?

W I'm ___________ ___________ ___________ my parents.

M That sounds nice. Do you see them often?

W ___________ ___________ ___________ ___________ I should. I always enjoy my visits, though.

M What do you like best about them?

W Well, I love my ___________ ___________. Every time I visit, she roasts a duck.

M Mm, that ___________ ___________.

W Oh, it is. Her roast duck is the best I've had.

Dictation

5

W For your birthday, I'm going to cook you _________ _________ _________.

M That sounds great! _________ _________ _________ anything I want?

W _________ _________! It's your birthday, after all.

M I think I want lobster tails. I _________ _________ _________ in a long time.

W OK. How do you like it prepared?

M You're _________ _________ _________ them in the oven.

W And how does one _________ _________ _________?

M Usually just with melted butter and _________ _________ _________ _________.

6

M Barbecue has a long tradition in the United States. _________ _________ _________ was made by poor people, who _________ _________ expensive meat. The meat that is used was once _________ _________ _________. For this reason, it was often _________. So in order to cook it, people had to slowly _________ _________ _________ low heat for a long time. After that, _________ _________ _________ and delicious, and easy to eat.

7

M I've always loved making things _________ _________ _________. It isn't always easy to build _________ _________ _________ _________, but it is always fun. I make _________ _________ _________ things. Chairs, tables, cabinets—no job is _________ _________ _________ _________. The most important thing to remember is _________ _________ _________. My father, who taught me to work _________ _________, always said, "Measure twice, cut once." In other words, you must be careful _________ _________ _________. This way, you never make a mistake, and the _________ _________ _________.

8

W Who is your _________ _________, Miguel?

M I like a lot of painters. But I think Monet is my favorite.

W Which of _________ _________ do you like the best?

M I can't remember the name of it. It features _________ _________, though.

W Oh yes, I know that one. A bridge over a _________, right?

M Yes, a small pond with _________ _________ in it.

W That is certainly a lovely painting.

M _________ _________ _________ see it. I hear it's in a museum in New York.

W Then we _________ _________ go there someday!

I'LL KEEP THAT IN MIND.

결심 말하기

나는 ~하기로 / ~하지 않기로 했어.	I've decided (not) to ~.
	I've decided (that) I should (not) ~.
그 말 꼭 기억할게.	I'll keep that in mind.
나는 ~하는 쪽을 선택했어.	I chose to ~.
나는 (~에 대한) 결정을 내렸어.	I made a decision (about ~).

기원하기

행운을 빌게.	I'll keep my fingers crossed for you. / All the best.
	Good luck (with ~). / Best of luck (with ~).
네가 ~하길 바랄게.	I hope you will ~.
즐거운 ~ 보내.	Have a good ~.

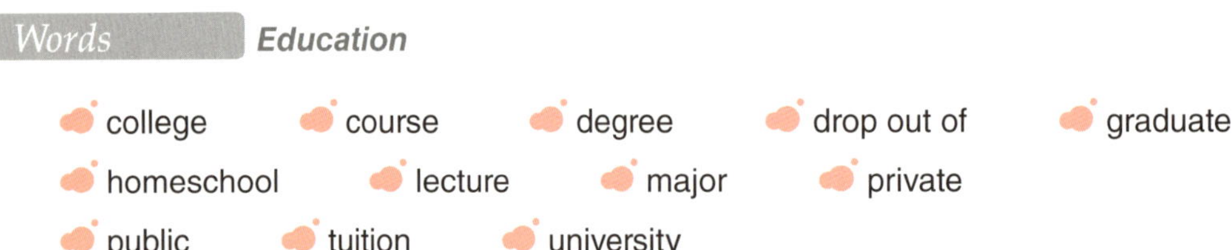

Words   *Education*

- college
- course
- degree
- drop out of
- graduate
- homeschool
- lecture
- major
- private
- public
- tuition
- university

01  다음 그림의 상황을 가장 잘 설명하는 문장을 고르세요.

02 대화를 듣고, 해당하는 것에 ✓ 표 하세요.

	Soccer	Basketball
More exciting		
Very challenging		
More popular		

03 주어진 표현을 사용하여 대화를 완성하세요.

I've decided to	all the best	keep that in mind	I hope you can

A ________________ study literature when I go to university.

B ________________ find a job after you graduate. It might be difficult.

A Well, I'll ________________. But I'm sure I'll be OK.

B All right. I wish you ________________ in the future.

들려주는 내용을 잘 듣고 물음에 답하세요.

1 대화를 듣고, 대화의 내용과 일치하는 것을 고르세요.

① 여자는 LA에 살고 있다.
② 남자는 영화배우를 보고 싶어 한다.
③ 여자는 사촌 집을 방문할 계획이다.
④ 남자는 여름 캠프에 갈 예정이다.
⑤ 여자는 남자의 계획에 무관심하다.

2 대화를 듣고, 두 사람의 관계로 가장 적절한 것을 고르세요.

① student – student
② son – mother
③ student – teacher
④ principal – teacher
⑤ teacher – teacher

3 다음을 듣고, 어디에서 들을 수 있는 내용인지 고르세요.

① 병원　　　② 녹음실　　　③ 박물관　　　④ 군대　　　⑤ 교실

4 다음 그림의 상황에 가장 잘 어울리는 대화를 고르세요.

①　　　　②　　　　③　　　　④　　　　⑤

5 다음을 듣고, 남자가 편지를 쓴 목적을 고르세요.

① 비판　　　② 초대　　　③ 불평　　　④ 위로　　　⑤ 축하

6 대화를 듣고, 여자의 심정으로 가장 적절한 것을 고르세요.

① content　　　② frustrated　　　③ excited
④ surprised　　　⑤ nervous

7 대화를 듣고, 아래 포스터에서 잘못된 것을 고르세요.

8 다음을 듣고, 내용과 일치하지 않는 것을 고르세요.

① 여자는 어렸을 때 홈스쿨링을 시작했다.
② 여자의 부모님은 공교육을 좋아하지 않는다.
③ 여자의 부모님은 딸이 말썽에 휘말리는 것을 원치 않는다.
④ 여자는 여전히 친구들을 만난다.
⑤ 여자는 십대가 되면 공립 학교로 돌아갈 예정이다.

다음을 듣고 빈칸에 들어갈 알맞은 말을 쓰세요.

1
W So, are you __________ __________ __________ this summer?
M No, I'm __________ __________ __________ in Los Angeles.
W That's so exciting. __________ __________ __________ __________ there?
M I want to __________ __________ __________ of Hollywood, for sure.
W Maybe you'll see some famous __________ __________.
M I hope so! That would be great!
W Well, __________ __________ __________ __________ your trip. Have fun!
M Thanks. I __________ __________!

2
M Mrs. Martin, __________ __________ __________ if we talk?
W Sure. How can I help you, Eric?
M Well, I __________ __________ I'm not doing well in your class.
W __________ __________ __________. Is there any way I can help?
M I don't know. I'm starting to think it's just too difficult.
W I understand. Maybe you should take __________ __________ in class.
M That's a good idea. I think I've __________ __________ __________ __________ to do that.
W Good. With a little hard work, I know you'll do fine.

3
W OK, class, we will be talking about ancient cultures. Who can tell me the __________ __________ Ancient Rome and Ancient Greece? For one thing, Rome was a larger state, with a great army. Greece, __________ __________ __________ __________, was a collection of small states. And they focused on the arts __________ __________ __________ and violence. You should be __________ __________, by the way. I've __________ __________ give a quiz on this later.

4
① W This is the best computer game ever!
　 M I'm glad you like it! __________ __________ __________ __________ buy it?
② M I need a new computer to use at college.
　 W This model here is very __________ __________ __________.
③ W Can you direct me to the computer department?
　 M Of course. It's __________ __________ __________, on the left.
④ M I wish __________ __________ __________ a new computer.
　 W Maybe you can get a __________ job and earn the money.
⑤ W I've __________ __________ __________ __________ to buy this television.
　 M You made an __________ __________. It's one of our best.

Dictation

5

M Dear Miss Green,

Thank you for being in our ______________ ____________. The judges really ____________

____________ ____________ ____________. Unfortunately, you did not win. However, your

writing shows a lot of ____________ for someone as young as you. As a result, we

____________ ____________ ____________ ____________ ____________ the awards ceremony. There,

you can read your wonderful poetry ____________ ____________ ____________. We hope you

will attend, and we ____________ ____________ ____________ ____________ ____________.

6

M Hey, Marcy. ____________ ____________ ____________?
W I'm working on an essay for ____________ ____________ ____________, and I can't find the
research I need at the library.
M Maybe you should ____________ ____________ ____________ to help.
W I tried that. They can't do anything for me.
M I don't know ____________ ____________ to tell you.
W It's ____________. I'm going to get an F, I just know it.
M Hey, don't worry. There must be something ____________ ____________ ____________.
W Maybe. I'm just ____________ ____________ ____________ the whole thing.

7

M Hey, Jen. Are you coming to quiz night?
W ____________ ____________ ____________ ____________ study tonight instead.
M Really? It's going to be great. You can ____________ ____________ ____________, like food and
drinks and prizes.
W Sounds great. It's at the Old Town Restaurant, right?
M Yes, from 7:30 – 9:30 every ____________ night.
W Every week, huh? Well, how about I come next week?
M That'd be great. Oh, and students ____________ ____________ ____________, by the way.

8

W My parents began to homeschool me at ____________ ____________ ____________. They don't like
a lot of what teachers teach in ____________ ____________. Also, they don't want me to be
around kids who might ____________ ____________ ____________ ____________. Home school isn't so
bad. I don't get to see my friends every day, but I ____________ ____________ ____________ on
the weekends. My parents say that when I am a teenager, I can ____________ ____________
go back to a public school if I want. But I ____________ ____________ whether I want to or not.

XI

HAVE YOU EVER BEEN ON A DIET?

경험 묻기

너 ~해본 적 있니?	Have you (ever) ~?
이번이 처음 ~하는 거니?	Is this your first time ~?
얼마나 여러 번 ~해봤니?	How many times have you ~?

답하기

응, 해봤어. / 아니, 해본 적 없어.	Yes, I have. / No, I haven't.
(사실은) ~을 여러 번 해봤어.	(Actually,) I've ~ many times.
이번이 처음 ~하는 거야.	This is my first time ~.
~해본 적이 한 번도 없어.	I've never ~.
~ 안 해봤지만 언젠가 해보고 싶어.	I haven't ~, but I want to someday.

Words   *Appearance*

- attractive
- be/go on a diet
- be satisfied with
- clothing
- envy
- gain/lose weight
- good-looking
- make-up
- neat
- skinny

01 그림의 상황에 가장 잘 어울리는 대화를 고르세요.

02 대화를 듣고, 내용과 일치하면 T, 일치하지 않으면 F에 ✓ 표 하세요.

1 The man has been to many fashion shows.　T　F
2 The man is invited to a fashion show.　T　F
3 The woman is going to a fashion show.　T　F

03 주어진 표현을 사용하여 대화를 완성하세요.

I've never been	your first time	How many times

A _________________ have you been to the theater?
B Actually, _________________ before.
A Oh, is this _________________? You must be excited.
B Yes, I've always wanted to go.

들려주는 내용을 잘 듣고 물음에 답하세요.

1 다음을 듣고, 여자가 오늘 한 일이 <u>아닌</u> 것을 고르세요.

2 대화를 듣고, 여자가 남자에게 부탁한 일을 고르세요.

① 음식점 예약하기 ② 다른 음식점에 가기 ③ 음식점에 메뉴 문의하기
④ 음식 배달시키기 ⑤ 화장품 가져다 주기

3 다음을 듣고, 여자의 주장으로 가장 적절한 것을 고르세요.

① 몸에 좋은 음식을 가려 먹어야 한다. ② 자신의 외모에 만족해야 한다.
③ 내면적인 변화를 추구해야 한다. ④ 다른 사람들과 같아지도록 노력해야 한다.
⑤ 개성 있는 옷차림을 연출해야 한다.

4 대화를 듣고, 아래 성적표에서 <u>잘못된</u> 것을 고르세요.

Report Card

Sam Smith

① Science	② Math	③ History	④ English	⑤ Art
C	A	C-	A-	B

5 대화를 듣고, 남자의 문제가 무엇인지 고르세요.

① 미식축구를 잘 하지 못한다.　　② 음식을 너무 많이 먹는다.

③ 미식축구 연습을 할 시간이 부족하다.　　④ 미식축구 팀에 들어가지 못했다.

⑤ 몸무게가 충분히 나가지 않는다.

* linebacker: 상대팀 선수들에게 태클을 걸며 방어하는 수비수

6 다음 상황 설명을 듣고, Jake가 할 말로 가장 적절한 것을 고르세요.

Jake

① I think I'm lost.

② Is this the high school?

③ Hi, my name is Jake.

④ Are you new here?

⑤ We should get to class.

7 대화를 듣고, 대화의 내용과 일치하는 것을 고르세요.

① 여자는 Harry Potter 영화를 좋아하지 않는다.

② 남자는 영화 보러 가는 것을 싫어한다.

③ 두 사람이 좋아하는 영화의 종류가 매우 다르다.

④ 남자가 가장 좋아하는 영화는 Harry Potter 시리즈이다.

⑤ 여자는 Harry Potter 시리즈 영화를 빠짐없이 보았다.

8 대화를 듣고, 여자가 다이어트를 하고 싶어 하는 이유를 고르세요.

① 모델처럼 날씬해지고 싶어서　　② 최근에 살이 너무 많이 쪄서

③ 친구들이 뚱뚱하다고 놀려서　　④ 헬스 클럽 트레이너가 권해서

⑤ 건강에 도움이 될 것 같아서

다음을 듣고 빈칸에 들어갈 알맞은 말을 쓰세요.

1

W Dear Diary: Today was __________ __________ __________ __________. First, I took a __________ __________ with my dog, Spot. We went to the park and played. Then __________ __________ __________ on the grass for a __________ __________. I saw some of my friends there, too, so we __________ __________ __________ of Frisbee afterward.

2

M Are you ready to __________ __________ __________ dinner, Rosa?
W Not quite yet.
M OK, I can wait. __________ __________ __________ been to this restaurant?
W No, it's my __________ __________. What's it like?
M Oh, you're going to love it. They have the best fish.
W Cool. What about __________ __________?
M I think they have them, but I'm not sure.
W You might want __________ __________ them and __________.
M Sure, I'll do that while you're getting ready.

3

W Have you ever wanted to __________ __________? Lots of young people are not happy with __________ __________ __________ __________. Sometimes, this can become very __________. For example, some people __________ __________ to be thin. But this can cause serious __________ __________, and even death. It's much better to just __________ __________ __________ the way you look. You are special and unique. Why try to __________ __________ __________ __________?

4

W Sam, we need to talk about __________ __________.
M I know. They aren't very good right now.
W According to your report card, you got a C __________ __________.
M I __________ __________ on the exams. But I'll study more. But I did get an A __________ __________.
W That's good. But you still need to __________ __________ in other classes, like history. You got a C⁻!
M You're right; I'll do better. But __________ __________ __________ my English grade.
W An A- is very good. As is an A in Art class. I guess I can't be __________ __________.
M I promise my grades __________ __________.

5

W Are you __________ __________ __________ the football team this year?
M Yes. In fact, tryouts are next week.

W ________ ________ then. What position do you want to play?
M I want to be a linebacker, but I don't think I can.
W And ________ ________ ________?
M I need to ________ ________ ________, I think.
W Yes, if you want to play defense, you have ________ ________ ________.
M Yeah. I think I'm just ________ ________ for it.
W Have you ________ ________ a lot?
M I think that's what I'll ________ ________ ________.

6
M It was Jake's ________ ________ of high school. Jake had ________ ________ ________ a real high school before. He had only been to home school ________ ________ ________. So when his parents decided to put him in a ________ ________, he was very nervous. To make things easier, he decided to make a ________ ________. He found someone who ________ ________ and approached him. In this situation, what will Jake say?

7
W Hey, Chris. What's your ________ ________?
M I love all the "Harry Potter" movies the best.
W Really? ________ ________ ________ have you seen them?
M ________ ________ ________ I can count.
W Well, I envy you. I like them too, but ________ ________ ________ see them all.
M Oh, you simply must! They are ________ ________ ________.
W Maybe we can watch them together sometime.
M That ________ ________ a lot of fun.

8
W ________ ________ ________ been on a diet, Mike?
M I was ________ ________ ________ a few years ago. Why?
W I just started one. This is my ________ ________ ________ ________.
M Oh. Why would you need to be on a diet?
W I just ________ ________ ________ a little bit of weight.
M But you look great already!
W You're very sweet, but I want to be ________, like the models on TV.
M If you ask me, ________ ________ ________. You're great just ________ ________ ________ ________.

XII UNIT
WHAT WOULD YOU DO IF YOU WERE PRESIDENT?

상상하여 묻기

만약 ~라면 넌 무엇을 하겠니?	What would you do if ~?
~하기 위해 넌 무엇을 하겠니?	What would you do to ~?

답하기

(만약 내가 ~라면) 나는 ~하겠어.	(If I were …,) I would ~.
나는 ~할 것 같아.	I would ~, I think.

상상하여 말하기

~했으면 좋겠다.	I wish ~.
그는 마치 ~인 것처럼 행동해.	He acts as if ~.
~이 없다면 나는 ~할 거야.	Without ~, I would ~.
~이 없었다면 나는 ~하지 못했을 거야.	I couldn't have ~ without ~.

Words   *Community*

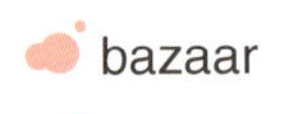 bazaar   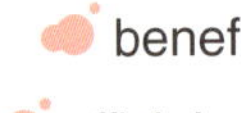 benefit    care    charity   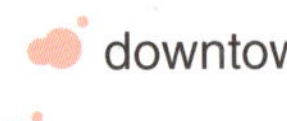 downtown   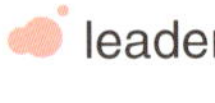 leader

 local    official    rural    service   support   urban

01 대화를 듣고, 언급되지 않은 활동을 고르세요.

02 다음을 듣고, 해당하는 것에 ✓ 표 하세요.

	Rural	Urban
Where many, many people live		
Where farms are located		
Where a lot of business takes place		

03 주어진 표현을 사용하여 대화를 완성하세요.

If I were	What would you	I would	I wish

A Hey, John. _________________ do if you were president?

B _________________ president, _________________ make every day
a holiday!

A Wow, _________________ you really were the president!

들려주는 내용을 잘 듣고 물음에 답하세요.

1 대화를 듣고, 여자의 장래 희망을 고르세요.

① 판사　　　　　　② 공무원　　　　　　③ 기자
④ 인권활동가　　　⑤ 사회복지사

2 대화를 듣고, 아래 포스터에서 <u>잘못된</u> 부분을 고르세요.

3 대화를 듣고, 두 사람이 이용할 교통수단을 고르세요.

① boat　　　　　② train　　　　　③ plane
④ subway　　　　⑤ bus

4 다음을 듣고, 무엇에 관한 내용인지 고르세요.

① Farms outside the city　　　② Growing crops in the city
③ How to find fresh vegetables　　④ Where the best markets are
⑤ Helping one's community

5 대화를 듣고, 두 사람이 만날 시각을 고르세요.

① 5:30　　　　② 6:00　　　　③ 6:30
④ 7:00　　　　⑤ 7:30

6 다음을 듣고, 이 글을 어디에서 볼 수 있는지 고르세요.

① 자원봉사 체험 수기
② 지역 신문
③ 자선단체 홍보 책자
④ 환경 관련 잡지
⑤ 가정통신문

7 대화를 듣고, 여자가 하는 자원봉사가 무엇인지 고르세요.

① 자선단체 홍보 활동
② 지역 주민을 위한 교육 참여
③ 노인들을 위한 행사 조직
④ 독거 노인 방문
⑤ 저소득층을 위한 모금 활동

8 다음 중 짝지어진 대화 중 어색한 것을 고르세요.

①　　　　②　　　　③　　　　④　　　　⑤

1

W I think I want to be ________ ________ ________ one day.
M It's a lot of hard work, but I'm sure you can do it.
W Thanks. I've always been ________ ________ ________.
M What would you do if you became an official?
W I ________ ________ ________ people's rights, I think.
M That's a very noble cause. ________ ________ ________ your dream!

2

M Hey, Lisa. You should come to the ________ ________ this Sunday.
W OK. What's the charity for?
M It's to ________ ________ ________. You can donate food, clothes, or toys.
W Hm. I don't know ________ ________ ________.
M Well, ________ ________ ________ ________ if you were poor?
W I'll think about that. What time is the event?
M It's from 9:00 – 11:00 at the ________ ________.
W OK. I'll see you there. Want to ________ ________ ________ afterward?
M ________ ________. There will be free hotdogs for everyone.

3

W I can't wait to visit our family this weekend!
M Me too. ________ ________ ________ ________ do it more often.
W Do you have our tickets?
M Yes, I have them here. They are ________ ________, like we asked.
W Great. And what time ________ ________ ________?
M The departure time is ________.
W So we should be there ________ ________ ________.
M That's a good idea. We'll have to search ________ ________ ________.
W I hope I don't get ________ ________, like last time!

4

M Most farms are found ________ ________ ________ cities. This means that fruit and vegetables are more expensive and ________ ________ in the city. Well, a few years ago I ________ ________ do something to help this. I planted a garden ________ ________ ________ of my apartment building. Since then, I've helped others ________ ________ ________. Now, there is ________ ________ ________ for fresh, local vegetables. Still, ________ ________ more people would ________ ________ ________.

Dictation

5

W Hey, Simon. Are you going to the concert tonight?

M ________ ________ ________ if I didn't have so much homework.

W You should really try. It's ________ ________, after all.

M I'll ________ ________ ________. What time does it start?

W It begins at ________.

M OK. How about meeting ________ ________ ________?

W That's not so good. I'm helping ________ ________ ________.

M OK. I'll find you a ________ ________ the concert then.

W Great! I hope to see you there.

6

W Today, two young boys were given an award ________ ________ ________ to the community. For months, the boys have been ________ ________ ________ from the roads and sidewalks in our town. They say that ________ ________ ________, but the real reward is helping ________ ________ ________ ________.

7

M I hear you've been doing ________ ________, Jan.

W Yes. Some friends and I started a program for ________ ________.

M That's very kind of you. What do you do?

W We ________ ________ for them at the community center.

M Neat. It's really important to take care ________ ________ ________.

W I agree. And we've gotten ________ ________ ________ ________ from the community.

M Really?

W Yes. We ________ ________ ________ it without their help.

M Well, best of ________ ________ ________.

8

① M Would you like to join me for a nice dinner downtown?

   W ________ ________ ________ I didn't have to work late tonight.

② M What would you do ________ ________ ________ rich?

   W No, I don't make much money at my job.

③ M I hear there is a ________ ________ at the park today.

   W We should go! ________ ________ ________ the community.

④ M Did you enjoy the book that I lent you?

   W It was so good that I read ________ ________ ________ in a day.

⑤ M What's the matter with Cathy? ________ ________ ________.

   W I know. She ________ ________ ________ everyone dislikes her.

Memo

Memo

Memo

Memo

Answer & Script

센치한 Listening 길들이기

감성 맞춤 내신 공략

내신 만점을 향한 중등 영어 듣기 기본서

- 최신 개정 교육과정 분석 및 필수 의사소통 기능 수록
- 실제 영어 듣기평가와 가장 가까운 문제 유형 및 소재 제시
- 효과적인 1일 학습량 제시
- 다시 한 번 확인하는 Dictation 코너
- 시·도 교육청 듣기평가 대비 실전 모의고사 3회 수록

마무리 **2**

센치한 Listening 길들이기

감성 맞춤 내신 공략

마무리 **2**

woongjin compass

UNIT 1 WHAT SHOULD I DO?

Check Up

01 c **02** 1.F 2.T 3.T

03 **A** I'm thinking about planting a garden. <u>Do you think I should</u> do it?

B Sure. I have one, and it's a great hobby. <u>I suggest that you</u> try it.

A OK. <u>Could you give me some tips</u> on starting a garden?

B <u>Why don't you</u> read a few books about gardening first?

Check Up Scripts

01

W Hi, John. Is that your new puppy?

M Actually, it's lost. I found it this morning.

W Look at its cute little spots!

M Yeah, and its big friendly smile.

W It's so cute!

M I know. What should I do with it?

W I suggest trying to find its real owner.

M That's a good idea. I'll ask my neighbors.

여 안녕. John. 그거 네 새 강아지니?

남 사실은 길 잃은 강아지야. 오늘 아침에 발견했어.

여 귀여운 작은 점들 좀 봐!

남 그래. 그리고 활짝 웃는 상냥한 미소도.

여 너무 귀엽다!

남 알아. 내가 어떻게 해야 할까?

여 진짜 주인을 찾으려고 노력해봐야 할 것 같아.

남 그거 좋은 생각이다. 이웃들한테 물어볼게.

Vocabulary	puppy 강아지 spot 점 suggest 권하다 owner 주인 neighbor 이웃

02

W What are you doing this summer?

M My grandfather invited me to work on his farm.

W I think you should do it. What's it like there?

M It's really big, and he grows a lot of crops, like corn and tomatoes.

W That's neat. I hope you enjoy it.

M It will be hard work, but I'm looking forward to it.

여 너 이번 여름에 뭐 할 거야?

남 할아버지가 농장에 와서 일하라고 하셨어.

여 너 그걸 해야 할 것 같아. 그곳은 어때?

남 정말 커. 그리고 할아버지는 옥수수나 토마토 같은 농작물을 많이 기르셔.

여 멋지다. 네가 즐기길 바랄게.

남 고된 일이겠지만 손꼽아 기다리고 있어..

Vocabulary	invite 초대하다 crop 농작물 neat 훌륭한, 깔끔한

03

A I'm thinking about planting a garden. Do you think I should do it?

B Sure. I have one, and it's a great hobby. I suggest that you try it.

A OK. Could you give me some tips on starting a garden?

A 난 정원을 만드는 것에 대해 생각 중이야. 내가 그래야 할 것 같니?

B 그럼. 나도 하나 있는데 아주 좋은 취미야. 너도 시도해 보기를 권해.

A 좋아. 정원을 시작하는 것에 대해 조언을 좀 해줄 수 있니?

B	Why don't you read a few books about gardening first?	B	우선 정원 가꾸기에 대한 책을 몇 권 읽어보지 그래?

Actual Test   1 ④   2 ②   3 ④   4 ②   5 ③   6 ④   7 ③   8 ③ | p.08

[The telephone rings.]	[전화벨 소리]
M What are you doing today, Layla? I thought we might <u>meet up</u> later.	남 오늘 뭐 해, Layla? 나중에 만나면 어떨까 생각했는데.
W I have some <u>errands to run</u>. I have to go to the gym, for one.	여 볼일이 좀 있어. 한 가지로, 헬스 클럽에 가야 해.
M That shouldn't take long. <u>What else</u> are you doing?	남 그건 오래 걸리지 않겠지. 다른 일은 뭘 하는데?
W After that I have to mail a few letters at the post office. Then I'm doing some grocery shopping.	여 그리고 나서는 우체국에서 편지를 몇 통 부쳐야 해. 그 다음에는 식료품을 좀 살 거고.
M OK. Can we meet after that?	남 그래. 그 후에 만날 수 있어?
W Almost. I just have to <u>pick up</u> my dry cleaning first.	여 거의. 먼저 세탁물만 찾으면 돼.
M OK. Why don't you just <u>give me a call</u> when you're done?	남 좋아. 그냥 볼일이 끝나면 전화 주는 게 어때?

M Are you coming to the play tonight? I have <u>a starring</u> role.	남 너 오늘 밤에 연극 보러 올 거야? 내가 주연을 맡았는데.
W Congratulations! That must be exciting.	여 축하해! 그거 신나겠다.
M Yes, but I'm a little nervous. Do you <u>have any tips</u>?	남 맞아, 하지만 약간 긴장돼. 조언 해줄 것이 있니?
W I suggest you don't worry <u>about the</u> audience.	여 관객에 대해서 걱정하지 않기를 권해.
M What do you mean?	남 무슨 뜻이야?
W Just <u>concentrate on</u> your performance. You'll be fine!	여 그냥 네 연기에 집중해. 넌 잘 할 거야!
M Thanks for <u>the advice</u>, Rose.	남 조언 고마워, Rose.
W Sure. I'll see you at the play tonight.	여 그래. 오늘 밤에 연극에서 보자.

3

W Today in Chicago, a bear escaped from the city zoo. So far, it has not been seen by anyone in the city. Workers from the zoo say that the bear is very dangerous. They suggest that you stay far away from the bear. And if you do see it, call the police. Above all, do not approach the wild animal for any reason. We'll bring you more information as the story develops.

여 오늘 시카고에서는 곰 한 마리가 시립 동물원에서 탈출했습니다. 지금까지 그것은 도시 안의 누구에게도 발견되지 않았습니다. 동물원 측에서는 그 곰이 매우 위험하다고 말합니다. 그들은 그 곰에게서 멀리 떨어져 있기를 권합니다. 그리고 그것을 보면 경찰에 신고하십시오. 무엇보다도, 어떤 이유로든 그 야생 동물에게 접근하지 마십시오. 이야기가 전개되는 대로 더 많은 소식을 전해드리겠습니다.

4

M My cat has been really sick lately.

남 내 고양이가 요즘 많이 아파.

W Really? What's wrong with him?

여 정말? 어디가 아픈데?

M Well, he is tired all the time. And he isn't eating.

남 음. 항상 피곤해해. 그리고 먹지를 않아.

W Why don't you take him to the vet?

여 수의사한테 데려가 보지 그래?

M I'm not sure if I can afford a doctor visit.

남 병원 진료 비용을 낼 수 있을지 모르겠어.

W It can be expensive. But isn't it worth it for your cat?

여 비쌀 수 있지. 하지만 네 고양이를 위해서라면 그만한 가치가 있지 않아?

M Well, he is my best friend. Maybe I can work a little extra to pay the bill.

남 음. 그는 내 제일 친한 친구야. 어쩌면 진료비를 내기 위해서 일을 더 할 수도 있어.

W Believe me, you'll be glad you did it when he's well again.

여 내 말 믿어. 그가 다시 건강해지면 넌 그러길 잘했다고 생각할 거야.

M You're right. Thanks for the talk, Gina.

남 네 말이 맞아. 이야기해 줘서 고마워, Gina.

5

W What is that you have there, Mike?

여 거기 네가 갖고 있는 게 뭐야, Mike?

M It's a bird's nest. I found it in my backyard last night.

남 새의 둥지야. 어젯밤에 우리 집 뒷마당에서 발견했어.

W Oh, it must have fallen from a tree.

여 오, 나무에서 떨어졌나 보구나.

M Yeah. Trouble is it had two small eggs in it.

남 응. 문제는 그 안에 작은 알이 두 개 들어있었던 거야.

W Why would a mother bird lay eggs and then abandon them?

여 왜 엄마 새가 알을 낳고서는 그것들을 버렸을까?

| M | I don't think it did. Maybe it got hurt or died. | 남 | 난 그랬다고 생각 안 해. 아마 다치거나 죽었겠지. |
| W | That could be. You'd better take good care of those eggs. | 여 | 그럴 수도 있겠다. 너 그 알들 잘 보살피는 게 좋겠다. |

| Vocabulary | nest 둥지   backyard 뒷마당   trouble 문제   lay (알을) 낳다   abandon 버리다   take care of ~을 돌보다 |

M	I can't wait for the City Arts Festival on Saturday.	남	토요일에 있을 시 예술 축제가 너무 기다려져.
W	I know; it's going to be great. We'll get to speak with real artists.	여	알아. 아주 좋을 거야. 진짜 예술가들과 말할 기회가 있을 거야.
M	Yeah. I'm thinking of entering the art contest, too. Should I do it?	남	그래. 난 예술 경연 대회에도 나가볼까 생각 중이야. 그래야 할까?
W	I really think you should. Your paintings are really good.	여	난 정말 네가 나가야 한다고 생각해. 네 그림은 정말 좋아.
M	Thanks. I'll bring my best one. Where do you want to meet?	남	고마워. 제일 좋은 작품으로 가져갈게. 어디서 만날까?
W	I'll meet you at City Plaza, where the festival is.	여	축제가 열리는 City Plaza에서 보자.
M	OK. I'll be at the entrance when the festival starts at 11:00.	남	그래. 축제가 시작하는 11시에 입구에 있을게.

| Vocabulary | festival 축제   artist 예술가   enter 참가하다   contest 대회   painting 그림   plaza 광장   entrance 입구 |

M	Is this your first time camping, Molly?	남	이번이 처음 캠핑하는 거니, Molly?
W	Yes. I'm having a lot of fun, though.	여	응. 하지만 아주 재미있어.
M	Me too. I do wish there were fewer insects.	남	나도야. 벌레가 좀 적었으면 정말 좋겠다.
W	Yeah, they're really annoying, especially when they bite.	여	그래. 정말 성가시다. 특히 물 때면.
M	I have some medicine for that, if you need it.	남	네가 필요하다면 나한테 벌레 쫓는 약이 있어.
W	That would be great. How do I use it?	여	그거 좋겠다. 어떻게 사용하는 거야?
M	I would spray it on your arms and legs. It will keep the bugs away.	남	팔다리에 뿌리는 거야. 벌레를 쫓아줄 거야.
W	Thanks, Jim! I'll do that right away.	여	고마워, Jim! 바로 해야겠다.

| Vocabulary | insect 곤충   annoying 성가신, 귀찮은   bite 물다   medicine 약   spray 뿌리다   keep away ~을 쫓다 |

① **M** How do I get rid of all these weeds?

W I suggest you pull them up by the roots.

② **M** How should I study for my English test?

W I recommend using note cards.

③ **M** What should I do with this old food?

W No, you relax while I cook dinner.

④ **M** Do you think I should try out for the team?

W Yes, I think you would have fun.

⑤ **M** Why don't you come to the movies with us?

W That sounds great. I need to have some fun.

① 남 이 잡초들을 어떻게 없애죠?

여 뿌리째 뽑을 것을 권해요.

② 남 영어 시험에 대비해서 어떻게 공부해야 할까?

여 노트 카드를 사용하는 걸 추천해.

③ 남 이 오래된 음식 어떻게 하지?

여 아냐, 내가 저녁을 요리하는 동안 넌 쉬어.

④ 남 넌 내가 팀에 지원해야 한다고 생각해?

여 응, 재미있을 것 같아.

⑤ 남 우리랑 같이 영화 보러 가지 않을래?

여 재미있겠다. 난 좀 즐겨야 해.

| Vocabulary | get rid of ~을 없애다 · weed 잡초 · recommend 추천하다 · relax 쉬다 · try out for ~에 지원하다 |

UNIX II WHAT DO YOU LIKE TO DO FOR FUN?

Check Up

p.13

01 b

02

	Coins	Comic Books
Can be worth more money	✓	
Can provide fun		✓
Are all unique	✓	

03 A Hi, Beth. What do you like to do for fun?

B Oh, I enjoy reading novels. What do you enjoy doing in your free time?

A I'm interested in literature as well. What's your favorite book?

B My favorite book is *The Great Gatsby*.

Check Up Scripts

01

M What do you like to do on the weekend, Jane?

남 넌 주말에 뭘 하는 걸 좋아해, Jane?

W	Oh, lots of things. I like hanging out with friends the most.	여	어, 많은 것들. 친구들이랑 어울려 노는 걸 제일 좋아해.
M	What do you and your friends enjoy doing?	남	너랑 네 친구들은 뭘 하는 걸 좋아하니?
W	Mostly, we watch videos together and eat popcorn.	여	주로 우린 같이 비디오를 보면서 팝콘을 먹어.
M	That sounds like fun!	남	그거 재미있겠다!

02

W	What do you enjoy doing in your free time?	여	넌 한가할 때 뭘 하는 걸 좋아하니?
M	I work on my hobby. I like to collect coins.	남	취미 활동을 해. 난 동전을 모으는 걸 좋아해.
W	Really? I collect things too. But I collect comic books.	여	정말? 나도 수집을 하는데. 하지만 난 만화책을 모아.
M	I prefer coins because they are all unique.	남	나는 동전이 저마다 독특하기 때문에 동전을 더 좋아해.
W	True, but comic books are fun to read.	여	사실이야. 하지만 만화책은 읽기에 재미있어.
M	You may be right. But old coins can be more valuable.	남	그럴 수도 있겠다. 하지만 옛날 동전들은 더 가치가 있어.

03

A	Hi, Beth. What do you like to do for fun?	A	안녕, Beth. 넌 뭘 하고 노는 걸 좋아하니?
B	Oh, I enjoy reading novels. What do you enjoy doing in your free time?	B	어, 나는 소설을 읽는 걸 좋아해. 너는 한가할 때 뭘 하는 걸 좋아하니?
A	I'm interested in literature as well. What's your favorite book?	A	나도 문학에 관심이 있어. 네가 제일 좋아하는 책은 뭐야?
B	My favorite book is *The Great Gatsby*.	B	내가 제일 좋아하는 책은 「위대한 개츠비」야.

Actual Test

1 ① 2 ④ 3 ④ 4 ③ 5 ⑤ 6 ③ 7 ⑤ 8 ② | p.14

1

M	Are you interested in history, Kate?	남	너 역사에 관심 있니, Kate?
W	Yes, I am fond of history. Why do you ask?	여	응, 난 역사 좋아해. 그건 왜 물어?
M	The city is offering a tour of historic places.	남	시에서 역사적인 장소를 둘러보는 투어를 제공한대.
W	Oh, that sounds like fun!	여	오, 그거 재미있겠다!
M	Yeah. They drive you around town and tell stories.	남	응. 그들이 운전해서 도시를 둘러보면서 이야기를 해 준대.
W	How interesting! Would you like to go together?	여	정말 흥미롭네! 같이 갈래?

M Yes, that would be great. Are you free
   Saturday?

W You bet. I'll see you then.

남 응, 그럼 아주 좋을 거야. 너 토요일에 한가해?

여 당연하지. 그때 보자.

| Vocabulary | be interested in ~에 관심이 있다   be fond of ~을 좋아하다   offer 제공하다
tour 투어, (도시, 건물 등을 둘러보는) 관광   historic 역사적인 |

2

W Are you going on the class trip next week?

M I didn't know there was one. Where is it?

W We are visiting a science lab for geology
   class.

M Oh, I do enjoy learning more about
   geology. But I might have plans already.

W Well, it's voluntary, so you don't have to
   come.

M I really want to, though. I'll look at my
   schedule.

W So will you come with us?

여 다음 주에 학급 여행 갈 거야?

남 학급 여행이 있는지 몰랐어. 어디로 가는데?

여 지리 수업에서 과학 실험실에 간대.

남 오, 난 지리에 대해서 더 많은 걸 배우는 게 정말 좋아. 하지만 이미 계획이 있을지 모르겠네.

여 음. 희망자만 참석하는 거라서 꼭 오지 않아도 돼.

남 근데 정말 가고 싶어. 일정을 확인해 봐야겠다.

여 그러면 같이 갈 거니?

| Vocabulary | class trip 학급 수학 여행   science lab 과학 실험실   geology 지리(학)   plan 계획   voluntary 자발적인
schedule 일정   definitely 꼭, 반드시 |

3

M We should do something to help the
   community.

W I agree. How about picking up litter in the
   park?

M That's a great idea. I have an interest in
   helping the environment.

W Me too. Let's meet at the park tomorrow at
   8:00.

M I'm going jogging at 8:00. How about
   meeting two hours later?

W My class starts at that time. But it only
   lasts an hour.

M Then we'll meet when your class is
   finished.

남 우린 지역사회를 돕기 위해 뭔가를 해야 해.

여 내 생각도 그래. 공원에서 쓰레기를 줍는 건 어떨까?

남 그거 좋은 생각이다. 난 환경을 돕는 것에 관심이 있어.

여 나도야. 내일 8시에 공원에서 만나자.

남 난 8시에 조깅을 하러 가. 두 시간 후에 만나면 어떨까?

여 그때 내 수업이 시작해. 하지만 한 시간밖에 안 걸려.

남 그러면 네 수업이 끝날 때 만나자.

| Vocabulary | community 지역사회   pick up 줍다   litter 쓰레기   have an interest in ~에 관심이 있다   environment 환경
last 지속되다 |

M I have always had a passion for cars. When I was a kid, I enjoyed reading magazines about sports cars and the like. My father taught me how to fix all kinds of car problems. By the time I was an adult, I knew all there was to know about fixing cars. It seemed natural that it would become my job one day. Now I get to do what I love all the time.

남 저는 언제나 차에 대한 열정이 있었습니다. 어릴 때 저는 스포츠카와 같은 것에 대한 잡지를 읽는 것을 좋아했어요. 아버지는 온갖 종류의 자동차 문제를 해결하는 방법을 제게 가르쳐 주셨습니다. 제가 성인이 되었을 무렵 저는 차를 고치는 것에 대해 모든 것을 알았습니다. 언젠가 그것이 제 일이 될 것이 당연하게 생각됐지요. 이제 저는 제가 사랑하는 일을 언제나 할 수 있습니다.

Vocabulary	passion 열정 magazine 잡지 and the like 그와 비슷한 것들 fix 고치다 adult 성인 natural 당연한, 자연스러운 mechanic 정비사 collector 수집가

[The telephone rings.]

W Hi, Jack. It's Marilyn.

M Hi, Marilyn. What's up?

W Well, you're keen on mountain climbing, right?

M You know I enjoy climbing mountains.

W I thought so. Are you aware of the big sale at the sports equipment store?

M No, I didn't know there was a sale going on.

W Oh, you must go. They have great deals on mountain climbing gear.

M That's great to hear. Thanks for letting me know.

[전화벨 소리]

여 안녕, Jack. 나 Marilyn이야.

남 안녕, Marilyn. 무슨 일이야?

여 음, 너 등산 좋아하지 않니?

남 너도 알다시피 난 등산을 즐기지.

여 그렇게 생각했어. 너 스포츠 용품점에서 큰 세일 하는 거 알고 있어?

남 아니, 세일을 하고 있는지 몰랐어.

여 오, 너 꼭 가봐야 해. 등산 장비가 아주 많아.

남 그거 좋은 소식이다. 알려줘서 고마워.

Vocabulary	be keen on ~을 무척 좋아하다 mountain climbing 등산 be aware of ~에 대해 알고 있다 equipment 장비 great deals 많은 양 gear 장비

M What do I enjoy in my free time? Well, I do have a favorite sport. It isn't for everyone. You have to be skilled at it to really have a good time. Also, you have to put up with harsh conditions, like cold weather, snow, ice, and other things. But for me, there's no sport like it. I love the feeling I get when I'm speeding down a mountain. I hit the slopes every opportunity I get.

남 제가 한가할 때 뭘 하는 걸 좋아하냐고요? 음, 저는 좋아하는 스포츠가 있답니다. 아무나 할 수 있는 건 아니에요. 정말 즐거운 시간을 보내려면 그것에 아주 능숙해야 하죠. 또 고된 여건도 견뎌야 합니다. 추운 날씨, 눈, 얼음, 그밖에 다른 것들 말이에요. 하지만 저에게 있어서 그것 만한 스포츠는 없습니다. 저는 산을 빠르게 내려올 때 느끼는 기분이 정말 좋습니다. 저는 기회가 있을 때마다 스키장에 가곤 합니다.

Vocabulary	skilled 능숙한 put up with ~을 견디다 harsh 고된 condition 여건, 조건 hit the slopes 스키를 타다 opportunity 기회

M Welcome to the Red Brick Cafe, where you'll find the best French food in the city. Are you <u>interested in</u> the five-course chef's menu? It <u>begins</u> with a fresh Caesar salad, followed by a hot bowl of rich French onion soup. We then serve you the <u>main course</u>, which is a beef roast with vegetables, followed by a plate of cheeses. Finally, for <u>dessert</u> we offer some delicious ice cream.

남 Red Brick Cafe에 오신 것을 환영합니다. 이곳에서 여러분은 이 도시에서 제일 가는 프랑스 음식을 발견하실 것입니다. 5단계 주방장 추천 메뉴에 관심이 있으신가요? 그것은 신선한 시저 샐러드로 시작해서, 뜨거운 그릇에 담긴 풍부한 프랑스 양파 수프로 이어집니다. 그러고 나서 메인 요리, 즉 야채를 곁들인 소고기 구이에 이어 치즈 요리가 서빙됩니다. 마지막으로 디저트로는 맛있는 아이스크림을 제공합니다.

Vocabulary	chef 주방장　　serve 서빙하다, (음식을) 내다　　plate 요리　　main course 주요리　　roast 구이　　dessert 디저트
	pastry 페이스트리

W Are you looking to <u>take up</u> a new hobby? Hobbies are a great way to <u>pass the time</u> and add more fun to your life! My favorite hobby is <u>caring for</u> my Bonsai tree. These beautiful plants can require <u>a lot of care</u>. But my new instructional video <u>makes it easy</u> for everyone! Order today to receive your own Bonsai and video, plus a <u>free gift</u> from me! Supply is limited; this offer won't <u>last long</u>!

여 새로운 취미를 시작하고자 하십니까? 취미는 시간을 보내고 여러분의 삶에 재미를 더하는 아주 좋은 방법이죠! 제가 제일 좋아하는 취미는 분재 나무를 가꾸는 것입니다. 이 아름다운 식물들은 많은 보살핌을 필요로 하지만 제가 만든 새로운 교육용 비디오는 그것을 모든 사람에게 쉽게 만들어 줍니다! 오늘 주문하셔서 여러분의 분재와 비디오, 그리고 제가 드리는 사은품을 받으세요! 공급량이 한정되어 있습니다. 이 기회는 오래 가지 않을 것입니다!

Vocabulary	take up (취미 등을) 시작하다　　pass the time 시간을 보내다　　care for ~을 돌보다　　plant 식물
	require 필요로 하다　　care 보살핌　　instructional 교육의　　supply 공급량　　limited 한정된　　offer 제공, 제안

UNIT III WHERE CAN I FIND
THE POST OFFICE?

Check Up

p.19

01 b **02** b, c

03 A <u>Where can I find</u> track 7B? I seem to be lost.

　B Go straight, then <u>turn left</u> at the news stand.

　A Great. <u>How long does it take</u> to get there? My train leaves in five minutes.

　B <u>It takes</u> a minute or two. You'll be fine.

01

W How far is it from here to the subway station?

M Not too far. From here, go to Park Street and take a left.

W OK, turn left at the park.

M Yes. Then take the first right, near the fire station.

W And that's where the subway station is?

M Yes, the first building on your right.

여 여기서 전철역까지 얼마나 멀어?

남 별로 멀지 않아. 여기서 Park Street로 가서 왼쪽으로 돌아.

여 알겠어. 공원에서 왼쪽으로 돌라고.

남 그래. 그러고 나서 첫 번째 길에서 우회전해. 소방서 근처야.

여 그리고 거기가 전철역이 있는 곳이야?

남 응. 오른쪽에 있는 첫 번째 건물이야.

Vocabulary	fire station 소방서

02

M Attention, class: There has been a change in the schedule today. I've decided to give the exam before the lecture instead of after. It will take about 45 minutes. But I will give you 15 minutes to study before the exam. Are there any questions?

남 여러분, 주목하세요. 오늘 일정에 변화가 생겼어요. 강의 후가 아니라 전에 시험을 보기로 했어요. 시험은 45분 정도 걸릴 거예요. 하지만 시험 전에 공부할 시간을 15분 드릴게요. 혹시 질문 있나요?

Vocabulary	attention 주의 decide 결정하다 lecture 강의

03

A Where can I find track 7B? I seem to be lost.

B Go straight, then turn left at the news stand.

A Great. How long does it take to get there? My train leaves in five minutes.

B It takes a minute or two. You'll be fine.

A 트랙 7B가 어디 있죠? 제가 길을 잃은 것 같아요.

B 쭉 가셔서 신문 가판대에서 왼쪽으로 가세요.

A 알겠어요. 거기까지 가는 데 얼마나 걸리나요? 제 기차가 5분 후에 떠나서요.

B 1~2분 걸려요. 괜찮으실 겁니다.

Vocabulary	track 트랙 news stand 신문 가판대

Actual Test   1 ④   2 ④   3 ②   4 ⑤   5 ③   6 ①   7 ④   8 ② | p.20

1

M I'm new to the city. <u>Where</u> <u>can</u> <u>I</u> <u>find</u> the post office?

W It's <u>about</u> <u>four</u> <u>miles</u> from here.

남 제가 이 도시에 온 지 얼마 안 됐어요. 우체국이 어디에 있나요?

여 여기서 4마일 정도 거리예요.

M OK. What's the best way to get there?

W You could get a taxi, but traffic is terrible.

M True. What about the bus?

W It's cheap, but you'd have to transfer a couple of times.

M Hm. It's too far to walk. I guess the subway is the fastest route.

남 알겠어요. 거기 가기에 제일 좋은 방법이 뭐죠?

여 택시를 타실 수 있지만 교통량이 너무 많네요.

남 맞아요. 버스는 어떤가요?

여 싸죠. 하지만 두어 번 갈아타셔야 할 거예요.

남 흠. 걷기엔 너무 멀고. 전철이 제일 빠른 길인 것 같네요.

traffic 교통량   terrible 아주 좋지 않은   transfer 갈아타다, 환승하다   route 길, 경로

2

W Hey, Jim. Are you going somewhere?

M Yes, I'm meeting my friend at the museum. How do I get there?

W The best route is to go north on Fifth Street, past the park.

M OK. Is the museum on Fifth Street?

W No, you have to turn right onto Green Avenue. The museum is on the opposite side of the street from City Hall.

M OK. How far is it to the museum from the school?

W Not far at all. It's about three miles.

M Great! Thanks for your help, Jan.

여 야, Jim. 어디 가는 길이야?

남 응. 박물관에서 친구를 만나기로 했어. 거기 어떻게 가니?

여 제일 좋은 경로는 공원을 지나서 5번가에서 북쪽으로 가는 거야.

남 알겠어. 박물관이 5번가에 있니?

여 아니. Green Avenue로 우회전해야 해. 박물관은 시청의 길 건너편에 있어.

남 알겠어. 학교에서 박물관까지 얼마나 멀어?

여 전혀 멀지 않아. 3마일 정도야.

남 좋아! 도와줘서 고마워, Jan.

past ~을 지나서   opposite 반대의, 반대쪽의

3

W Last summer, Claire took a vacation to Paris. She didn't know the city, so she wandered around looking at the sights. One day, she wandered too far and found that she was lost. She needed to get back to her hotel but didn't know the way. She located the nearest policeman to see if he could help her. In this situation, what will Claire say?

여 지난 여름, Claire는 파리로 여행을 갔다. 그녀는 그 도시를 몰라서 관광지를 보면서 그냥 돌아다녔다. 어느 날 그녀는 너무 멀리 가서 길을 잃었다는 것을 알았다. 그녀는 호텔로 돌아가고 싶었지만 길을 몰랐다. 그녀는 그녀를 도와줄 수 있는지 물어보기 위해 가장 가까이에 있는 경찰관을 찾아보았다. 이 상황에서 Claire는 뭐라고 말할까?

wander 돌아다니다, 거닐다   sights 명소, 관광지   locate ~의 위치를 찾다   crime 범죄

4

M Hello, ma'am. Where can I take you?

W I need to go downtown for a meeting.

M Sure, I can take you there.

남 안녕하세요, 부인. 어디로 모실까요?

여 회의가 있어서 시내에 가야 해요.

남 알겠습니다. 거기로 모실게요.

W	How long will it take to get to the Harris Building?	**여**	Harris Building까지 얼마나 걸릴까요?
M	In this traffic? Probably 20 minutes or more.	**남**	이 교통량에서요? 아마 20분이나 더 걸릴 수도 있고요.
W	But I thought it was just a couple of miles.	**여**	하지만 겨우 2마일 정도라고 생각했는데요.
M	It is. I only charge for distance, though, so the fare will be cheap.	**남**	그래요. 하지만 전 거리로만 요금을 받으니까 요금은 쌀 겁니다.

> **Vocabulary**   downtown 시내로, 시내에   charge (요금을) 청구하다   distance 거리   fare 요금

5

W	Attention all passengers on flight 1243. We are now boarding for our departure at 4:40. Please report to gate 32 to board your flight. That's flight 1243, nonstop to London. It will take about five and a half hours to reach our destination, where the local arrival time will be 3:10. Thank you.	**여**	항공편 1243을 이용하시는 승객 여러분께 알려드립니다. 4시 40분 출발을 위해 탑승을 진행 중입니다. 32번 게이트로 가셔서 항공편에 탑승하십시오. 런던으로 가는 직항 항공편 1243입니다. 목적지에 도착하기까지 5시간 반 정도 걸릴 예정입니다. 도착지의 현지 도착 시각은 3시 10분이 될 것입니다. 감사합니다.

> **Vocabulary**   passenger 승객   flight 항공편   board 탑승하다   departure 출발   report 보고하다   gate 문, 탑승구
> nonstop 직항으로   destination 목적지   local 현지의   arrival 도착

6

M	Hi. My name is Dr. James Wilson. A lot of people ask themselves, "Where can I find happiness?" They look for happiness in jobs, in relationships, in buying things. But I'm here to tell you that it's right in front of you already. In my new book *The Secret to Happiness*, you'll learn to find happiness in everyday things. So pick up a copy of my book today, and learn the real secret to happiness.	**남**	안녕하세요. 제 이름은 James Wilson 박사입니다. 많은 사람들이 스스로에게 묻습니다. "어디에서 행복을 찾아야 할까?" 그들은 일에서, 인간 관계에서, 물건을 사는 것에서 행복을 찾습니다. 하지만 저는 이 자리에서 여러분에게 행복은 이미 여러분 앞에 있다는 것을 말씀드리고자 합니다. 제 신간인 「행복의 비결」에서 여러분은 일상적인 것들에서 행복을 찾는 법을 배우실 것입니다. 그러니 오늘 제 책을 한 부 집어 드셔서 행복을 얻는 진짜 비결을 배우세요.

> **Vocabulary**   relationship 인간 관계   secret 비밀, 비결   pick up 집어 들다   copy (책, 잡지의) 부

7

M	Hey, Julie. What's the matter?	**남**	이봐, Julie. 무슨 일 있어?
W	I wrecked my car today. Another vehicle hit it on the freeway.	**여**	오늘 차 사고가 났어. 다른 차가 내 차를 고속도로에서 받았어.
M	Oh no! Well, I'm glad you aren't hurt.	**남**	오 저런! 음, 네가 다치지 않아서 다행이다.
W	Yeah, I guess so. Now I have to drive my parents' old car instead.	**여**	그래, 그런 것 같아. 이제 난 대신 부모님의 낡은 차를 운전해야 해.
M	At least you still have something to drive.	**남**	그래도 아직 운전할 것이 있긴 하잖아.
W	I know, I know. But it's an old person's car! It's embarrassing!	**여**	알아, 알아. 하지만 그건 나이든 사람들이 타는 차야! 창피해!

M	Just be grateful that you have a car at all.	남	그래도 차가 있다는 것에 감사해.
W	Yeah. I should count myself lucky, I guess.	여	그래. 운이 좋다고 생각해야겠지.
M	Sometimes you have to take whatever you can get.	남	때로는 그저 네게 주어지는 것을 갖는 수밖에 없어.

Vocabulary	wreck 차 사고를 내다 vehicle 차량 freeway 고속도로 at least 최소한 embarrassing 창피한
	grateful 감사하는 count ~라고 생각하다 hay 건초 end 끝내다; 목적 justify 정당화하다 means 수단
	beggar 거지 opportunity 기회

W	Hey, Paul. How long does it take to go to Orange Beach?	여	이봐, Paul. Orange Beach까지 가는 데 얼마나 걸려?
M	It takes an hour or two, depending on the type of transportation. Why?	남	한두 시간 걸려. 교통수단의 종류에 따라 다르지. 왜?
W	I thought you might want to join me at the coast this weekend.	여	네가 이번 주말에 나랑 같이 해안에 갈 수 있을까 생각하고 있었어.
M	That sounds like fun. How do you want to get there?	남	그거 재미있겠다. 거기에 어떻게 가고 싶어?
W	Well, we could get there by train. But there's a transfer.	여	음. 기차를 타고 갈 수도 있어. 하지만 갈아타야 해.
M	Oh, you're right. You can only get there via Central City.	남	오, 맞아. Central City를 경유해야만 거기에 갈 수 있어.
W	Still, it's probably shorter than driving. And cheaper.	여	그래도 운전하는 것보다는 아마 짧게 걸릴 거야. 더 싸기도 하고.
M	Great. I look forward to it.	남	좋았어. 기대된다.

Vocabulary	depending on ~에 따라 transportation 교통수단 coast 해안 transfer 환승 via ~을 경유하여

UNIT IV WHAT IS IT ABOUT?

 Check Up

p.25

01 a   **02** 1.T   2.F   3.F

03 A Do you know why your parents named you John?

    B I know that my grandfather's name is John. I think I'm named after him.

    A Oh, that's right. I think you have told me about that before.

    B Can you tell me where your name comes from?

01

a. **W** Can you tell me about this painting?

  M Yes. It's beautiful, isn't it?

b. **W** Want to go to the art museum?

  M No thanks. I find them boring.

c. **W** What a beautiful sculpture!

  M Yes, it is a great piece of art.

a. **여** 이 그림에 대해 말해줄 수 있어?

  남 응. 아름답지 않아?

b. **여** 미술관에 가고 싶어?

  남 고맙지만 사양할게. 난 미술관이 지루해.

c. **여** 정말 아름다운 조각이다!

  남 그래. 정말 훌륭한 예술 작품이야.

Vocabulary	painting 그림　boring 지루한　sculpture 조각　piece of art 예술 작품

02

M I got a haircut. Didn't you notice?

W Um, no. What was it like before?

M It was kind of long and messy.

W Well, I think it looks nice now.

M That's sweet of you to say.

남 나 머리 잘랐어. 눈치 챘니?

여 음, 아니. 전에는 어땠지?

남 좀 길고 지저분했지.

여 어, 지금은 좋아 보이네.

남 그렇게 말해줘서 고맙다.

Vocabulary	get a haircut 머리를 자르다　notice 눈치 채다, 알아차리다　messy 지저분한

03

A Do you know why your parents named you John?

B I know that my grandfather's name is John. I think I'm named after him.

A Oh, that's right. I think you have told me about that before.

B Can you tell me where your name comes from?

A 너는 왜 너희 부모님이 네 이름을 John이라고 지었는지 알아?

B 할아버지 성함이 John이라는 걸 알아. 내 생각에 그분 이름을 딴 것 같아.

A 오, 그렇구나. 전에 네가 그것에 대해 얘기해 준 적이 있는 것 같아.

B 네 이름은 어디서 왔는지 말해 줄래?

Vocabulary	name after ~을 따라 이름 짓다

Actual Test　　1 ①　2 ②　3 ④　4 ⑤　5 ①　6 ②　7 ③　8 ②　　| p.26

1

M Hey, Mom? Can I have some extra pocket money for the weekend?

W What do you need extra money for?

M To buy things, like a CD or a video game.

남 저기, 엄마? 주말 동안 쓸 용돈 좀 더 주실 수 있어요?

여 돈이 왜 더 필요한데?

남 물건 좀 사려고요. CD나 비디오 게임 같은 거요.

W You know I don't like you playing too many video games.

M But I also have no money to go out with friends.

W OK, let's make a deal. If you help me clean the house, I'll give you a little more money.

M Thanks, Mom! You're the best!

여 네가 비디오 게임 너무 많이 하는 거 내가 안 좋아하는 거 알잖니.

남 하지만 친구들과 나가 놀 돈도 없단 말이에요.

여 좋아. 이렇게 정하자. 네가 집 청소하는 걸 도우면 내가 돈을 좀 더 줄게.

남 고마워요, 엄마! 엄마가 최고예요!

| Vocabulary | extra 여분의, 추가의　pocket money 용돈　make a deal 거래하다, 계약하다 |

2

W I want this CD so bad! It's my favorite band.

M Well, why don't you buy it then?

W It's too expensive. I only have $5.

M Can you tell me about their music?

W Oh, it's the best. They play rock music.

M That sounds like something I would like, too.

W Do you want to buy it together?

M Sure, I have some money. We'll share it.

W That's very generous of you!

여 나 이 CD 너무 고 싶어! 내가 제일 좋아하는 밴드야.

남 어, 그럼 사지 그러니?

여 너무 비싸. 난 5달러밖에 없어.

남 그들의 음악에 대해 말해줄 수 있니?

여 오, 최고야. 록 음악을 연주해.

남 나도 좋아할 만한 것처럼 들리는데.

여 같이 사고 싶니?

남 그럼. 난 돈이 좀 있어. 우리 같이 공유하자.

여 정말 너그럽구나!

| Vocabulary | bad 심하게, 매우　share 공유하다　generous 너그러운, 후한 |

3

M For my class project, I asked my friends about their pocket money. Then I made this chart to show how much money they get each week. My friend Mark told me that he gets $10 a week from his parents. Judy, however, only gets half as much money as Mark. Billy and Kate get the most pocket money at $20 per week. And James receives $15 a week from his grandmother.

남 수업 프로젝트로 저는 제 친구들에게 그들의 용돈에 대해 물어보았습니다. 그리고 나서 그들이 매주 얼마나 많은 돈을 받는지 보여주기 위해 이 차트를 만들었습니다. 제 친구 Mark는 부모님으로부터 일주일에 10달러를 받는다고 말해주었습니다. 하지만 Judy는 Mark보다 반만 받습니다. Billy와 Kate는 주당 20달러로 가장 많은 용돈을 받습니다. 그리고 James는 할머니로부터 일주일에 15달러를 받습니다.

| Vocabulary | pocket money 용돈　receive 받다 |

4

W What do you want to be when you grow up, Michael?

M I want to be a lawyer. They make a really

여 넌 커서 뭐가 되고 싶어, Michael?

남 난 변호사가 되고 싶어. 그들은 아주 높은 연봉을 받잖아.

high <u>salary</u>.

W You mean they make a lot of money?

M Yeah, that's what salary is. It's <u>how</u> <u>much</u> <u>money</u> <u>you</u> <u>make</u>.

W Well, I want to be a <u>teacher</u> when I grow up.

M Really? <u>How</u> <u>come</u>?

W I like teaching people things. <u>It</u> <u>doesn't</u> <u>pay</u> a lot of money though.

M Yes, I know. Then why would you want to do it?

W <u>Because</u> I <u>like</u> <u>it</u>. To me, that's more important than money.

여	돈을 많이 번다는 뜻이니?
남	응, 그게 연봉의 의미야. 그건 돈을 얼마나 버는가 하는 거야.
여	음, 난 커서 선생님이 되고 싶어.
남	정말? 어째서?
여	난 사람들에게 뭔가를 가르치는 게 좋아. 돈은 별로 많이 받지 못하지만.
남	그래, 알아. 그런데 왜 그걸 하고 싶니?
여	내가 좋아하니까. 나에게는 그게 돈보다 더 중요해.

> **Vocabulary** lawyer 변호사   salary 연봉, 봉급   pay 지불하다

5

W <u>Hurry</u> <u>up</u>, Ken! You'll miss the bus!

M <u>I'm</u> <u>trying</u>, but I have a small problem.

W <u>What</u> <u>is</u> <u>it</u>? Maybe I can help.

M I can't find my <u>bus</u> <u>pass</u>. And I didn't bring any money.

W Uh-oh. They won't <u>let</u> <u>you</u> <u>on</u> the bus then.

M I know. Do you have any <u>extra</u> <u>change</u>?

W I can <u>lend</u> <u>you</u> a dollar, if you want.

M That'd be great. I'll <u>pay</u> <u>you</u> <u>back</u> tomorrow.

여	서둘러, Ken! 너 버스 놓치겠어!
남	노력 중이야. 하지만 문제가 있어.
여	뭔데? 어쩌면 내가 도와줄 수도 있잖아.
남	내 버스 카드를 못 찾겠어. 그리고 난 돈을 하나도 안 가져왔어.
여	저런. 그럼 버스에 태워주지 않을 텐데.
남	알아. 너 여분의 잔돈 있니?
여	원한다면 1달러 빌려줄 수 있어.
남	그럼 정말 좋겠다. 내일 갚을게.

> **Vocabulary** hurry up 서두르다   miss 놓치다   bus pass 버스 통행권, 버스 카드   extra 여분의   change 잔돈
> lend 빌려주다   pay back 갚다

6

M Do you want to be rich? <u>Sure</u> <u>you</u> do! Everyone wants to have <u>more</u> <u>money</u>. Well, today I'm going to tell you the <u>secret</u> <u>to</u> getting rich fast. It's all in my <u>new</u> <u>book</u>, called *More Money Now*! Do you know <u>what</u> <u>it</u> takes to be successful? Do you want to know the secrets of rich people? For the <u>low</u> <u>price</u> of $35, you get the answers to these questions and more. So call today and <u>buy</u> <u>my</u> books!

남 부자가 되고 싶으신가요? 물론 그러시겠죠! 모든 사람이 돈을 더 갖고 싶어 합니다. 음, 오늘 저는 빠르게 부자가 되는 비결을 여러분께 알려드리려고 합니다. 그것은 모두 「지금 더 많은 돈을!」이라는 제목의 제 새 책에 나와 있습니다. 성공하기 위해 무엇이 필요한지 아시나요? 부자들의 비결을 알고 싶으신가요? 35달러라는 저렴한 가격에 여러분은 이런 질문들에 대한 대답과 더 많은 것들을 얻으실 겁니다. 그러니 오늘 전화하셔서 제 책을 사세요!

> **Vocabulary** secret 비밀, 비결   successful 성공한   price 가격

7

W Good morning. How can I help you?

M I'd like to open an account, please.

W I'd be happy to help. Will that be checking or savings?

M I want to open a savings account.

W I just need you to fill out this paperwork.

M Of course. And I brought some money for my first deposit.

W Great. We'll have your account set up in just a moment.

여 안녕하세요. 무엇을 도와드릴까요?

남 계좌를 개설하고 싶습니다.

여 기꺼이 도와드리겠습니다. 당좌 예금 계좌인가요, 보통 예금 계좌인가요?

남 보통 예금 계좌를 개설하고 싶습니다.

여 이 서류만 작성해 주시면 되겠습니다.

남 그러죠. 그리고 첫 예치금으로 돈을 좀 가져왔습니다.

여 잘 하셨네요. 잠시 후에 계좌를 마련해 드리겠습니다.

Vocabulary	account 은행 계좌 checking account 당좌 예금 계좌 savings account 보통 예금 계좌 fill out 작성하다 paperwork 서류 deposit 예치금 currency exchange 환전소 courtroom 법정

8

① M Are you sure this is the correct building?

W It is the address I was given.

② M I think we should invest in the stock market.

W Sure, I'll go to the market with you.

③ M Do you know why the dinosaurs died?

W I hear there are a lot of theories, but no one really knows.

④ M My teacher has told me that I should talk more in class.

W I agree. You have some very smart things to say.

⑤ M It used to be easy to get good grades.

W I know. High school is so much harder!

① 남 이 건물이 확실히 맞아?

여 그게 내가 받은 주소야.

② 남 내 생각에 우린 주식 시장에 투자해야 할 것 같아.

여 좋아. 나도 너와 함께 시장에 갈게.

③ 남 너 공룡들이 왜 죽었는지 알아?

여 많은 이론이 있지만 정말로는 아무도 모른다고 들었어.

④ 남 선생님이 그러시는데 내가 수업시간에 말을 더 많이 해야 한대.

여 나도 그렇게 생각해. 넌 아주 똑똑한 말들을 할 게 있잖아.

⑤ 남 (예전에는) 좋은 성적을 받기가 쉬웠는데.

여 알아. 고등학교는 훨씬 더 어려워!

Vocabulary	correct 올바른, 정확한 invest 투자하다 stock market 주식 시장 dinosaur 공룡 theory 이론

UNIT V DO YOU MIND IF WE TALK ABOUT IT?

Check Up

01 c **02** b, c

03 A Is it okay if I borrow your textbook today?
B I'm afraid not. I need it to read during class.
A OK. Do you mind if I read along with you then?
B Not at all. That'd be fine.

Check Up Scripts

01

W Hey, Mike. What's wrong?

M My favorite pet died this weekend.

W Oh, I'm so sorry! You must feel terrible.

M Yeah, I'm really down. Do you mind if we talk about it?

W Of course not. It's always best to talk about your feelings.

여	안녕. Mike. 무슨 일 있어?
남	내가 제일 좋아하는 애완동물이 이번 주말에 죽었어.
여	오, 정말 안됐다! 너무 심란하겠어.
남	응. 정말 마음이 안 좋아. 그것에 대해서 이야기 좀 하면 안 될까?
여	물론 되고말고. 기분에 대해서 이야기하는 것이 항상 제일 좋아.

> **Vocabulary** terrible 끔찍한, 아주 좋지 않은 down 기분이 안 좋은

02

M Are you going anywhere for the holidays?

W I want to, but I've got a lot of work to do.

M So you'll be at home by yourself?

W Yeah, it looks that way.

M Well, feel free to come over to my house for dinner.

W I'd be delighted, Dan. Thank you.

남	연휴에 어디 갈 거니?
여	그러고 싶은데 할 일이 많아.
남	그럼 혼자 집에 있을 거야?
여	응. 그럴 것 같아.
남	음. 저녁 먹으러 우리 집에 얼마든지 와도 돼.
여	그럼 정말 기뻐. Dan. 고마워.

> **Vocabulary** holiday 휴일 feel free to 마음대로 ~하다 delighted 기쁜 curious 호기심이 많은, 궁금해하는

03

A Is it okay if I borrow your textbook today?

B I'm afraid not. I need it to read during class.

A OK. Do you mind if I read along with you then?

B Not at all. That'd be fine.

A	오늘 네 교과서를 빌려도 돼?
B	안 되겠는데. 수업시간에 읽어야 해서 필요해.
A	알았어. 그럼 네 걸 같이 읽어도 될까?
B	되고말고. 그건 괜찮아.

> **Vocabulary** borrow 빌리다 textbook 교과서

1

M What's the matter, Pam?

W I have a test on Friday, and I feel a bit anxious.

M Why so nervous? I'm sure you'll do fine.

W I haven't been listening much in class.

M That's not good.

W No, and my notes aren't so great either.

M I always take really careful notes.

W Do you mind if I borrow them, to study?

M I don't think that would be right.

남 무슨 일 있어. Pam?

여 금요일에 시험이 있는데 좀 걱정돼.

남 왜 그렇게 초조해해? 넌 분명 잘 할 거야.

여 수업시간에 잘 듣질 않았어.

남 그건 안 좋은데.

여 그래, 그리고 내 필기도 별로 좋지 않아.

남 난 항상 주의 깊게 필기를 하는데.

여 네 필기 좀 빌려도 될까. 공부하게?

남 그건 옳은 일이 아닐 것 같아.

Vocabulary	anxious 걱정되는 nervous 초조한 take notes 필기하다

2

M Greg was at a movie with his parents. He was having a lot of fun, until some people behind him started talking loudly during the film. He didn't want to move seats, but he was offended by all of their rude behavior. Greg turned around to face the loud people. In this situation, what would Greg say?

남 Greg는 부모님과 함께 영화관에 있었다. 그는 아주 재미있게 즐기고 있었는데 그의 뒤에 앉은 사람들이 영화 상영 중에 시끄럽게 떠들기 시작했다. 그는 자리를 옮기고 싶지 않았지만 그들의 무례한 행동으로 기분이 상했다. Greg는 뒤돌아서 그 시끄러운 사람들을 마주보았다. 이 상황에서 Greg는 뭐라고 말하겠는가?

Vocabulary	loudly 시끄럽게 seat 좌석 offend 기분을 상하게 하다 rude 무례한 behavior 행동 turn around 뒤돌다 face 마주보다

3

W My job requires me to be very confident. I have to talk to new people all the time, and I need them to trust me. It is my job to make them believe that they need to buy what I have. If they don't trust me, then they likely won't want to buy anything from me. All in all, I'm pretty good at my job, and it still feels great to make a sale.

여 제 일은 제가 아주 자신감이 넘치기를 요구합니다. 저는 항상 새로운 사람들에게 이야기를 해야 하고 그들이 저를 믿도록 해야 합니다. 제가 갖고 있는 것을 사야 한다고 그들이 믿게 만드는 것이 제 일입니다. 그들이 저를 신뢰하지 못하면 그들은 저에게서 어떤 것도 사고 싶어 하지 않을 것입니다. 대체로 저는 제 일을 썩 잘 합니다. 그리고 판매를 할 때 느끼는 기분은 여전히 아주 좋습니다.

Vocabulary	require 요구하다 confident 자신감 있는 trust 믿다, 신뢰하다 likely 아마도 all in all 대체로 pretty 꽤, 썩 make a sale 판매하다

M Excuse me, ma'am? <u>May</u> <u>I</u> <u>ask</u> you a question?

W <u>Of course</u>. What is it?

M When will flight 113 arrive?

W Oh yes. The flight was <u>delayed</u> a bit. It was supposed to arrive at 4:00. It was an hour late leaving Los Angeles.

M OK. Are there any other problems?

W Also, because of the storms, the plane could take an <u>extra</u> <u>30</u> <u>minutes</u> to land.

M Thank you, I'm very <u>grateful</u> for your help.

W It's no trouble, sir.

남	실례합니다? 질문 좀 드려도 될까요?
여	그럼요. 무슨 일이시죠?
남	항공편 113이 언제 도착하나요?
여	아 네. 그 항공편은 조금 지연되었어요. 4시에 도착하기로 되어 있었죠. 로스앤젤레스를 떠날 때 한 시간이 늦었어요.
남	알겠습니다. 다른 문제도 혹시 있나요?
여	또 폭풍우 때문에 비행기가 착륙하는 데 30분이 더 걸릴 수 있습니다.
남	감사합니다. 도와주셔서 정말 감사합니다.
여	천만에요.

Vocabulary	flight 항공편 delay 지연시키다 extra 추가의 land 착륙하다 grateful 감사하는 trouble 수고

M I'm looking for a present for my niece.

W Oh? <u>What's</u> <u>the</u> <u>occasion</u>?

M Last week was her birthday. <u>I</u> <u>feel</u> <u>guilty</u> for missing it.

W Well, we have a great <u>selection</u> <u>of</u> <u>jewelry</u>.

M I don't have much money, actually.

W How about <u>a nice dress</u>?

M I'm afraid I don't know her size.

W You could always buy her a <u>gift</u> <u>certificate</u>.

M I want to get something <u>more</u> <u>personal</u>.

W Over here, we have <u>a nice collection</u> of winter scarves and gloves.

M Oh, those look nice. I think she'll be content with a <u>colorful</u> <u>scarf</u>.

W OK. Can I <u>wrap that up</u> for you?

남	여자 조카에게 줄 선물을 찾고 있어요.
여	오? 어떤 선물을 하시려고요?
남	지난주가 그 애 생일이었어요. 챙겨주지 못해서 죄책감이 들어요.
여	음, 저희는 엄선된 다양한 보석 제품들이 있습니다.
남	사실 돈이 별로 많지 않아요.
여	새 드레스는 어떤가요?
남	사이즈를 몰라서요.
여	언제든 상품권을 주실 수도 있죠.
남	좀 더 개인적인 것을 주고 싶어요.
여	이쪽에 겨울 목도리와 장갑 제품이 잘 구비되어 있습니다.
남	오, 그것들 예쁘네요. 그 애가 알록달록한 목도리를 마음에 들어 할 것 같아요.
여	알겠습니다. 포장해 드릴까요?

Vocabulary	niece 여자 조카 occasion 경우, 때 guilty 죄책감이 드는 selection 선택된 것들 jewelry 보석 gift certificate 상품권 personal 개인적인 collection 모음 scarf 스카프, 목도리 glove 장갑 content 만족한 wrap up ~을 포장하다

M ① The boy is playing <u>outdoors</u> with his dog.

   ② The children are building a <u>sand castle</u>.

남	① 소년이 야외에서 개와 놀고 있다.
	② 아이들이 모래성을 짓고 있다.

③ The girl is frightened of the mouse.

④ The boy is playing an electric guitar.

⑤ The kids are eating ice cream together.

③ 소녀가 쥐 때문에 겁에 질려 있다.

④ 소년이 전기 기타를 연주하고 있다.

⑤ 아이들이 함께 아이스크림을 먹고 있다.

7

M The alarm clock went off, and I sat up in bed. I looked at the clock. It was already 7:30, and I had to catch my bus at 8:00. I panicked! I couldn't be late for class again. I'd be so ashamed! So I took the fastest shower that I could, threw on some clothes, grabbed my bag, and ran for the bus stop. Just as I arrived, the bus was driving off. I yelled, "Please, let me on the bus!" And surprisingly, it stopped. I got on it and sat down. My worries were over.

남 알람 시계가 울렸고 나는 침대에 일어나 앉았다. 나는 시계를 보았다. 벌써 7시 30분이었고 나는 8시 버스를 타야 했다. 나는 어쩔 줄을 몰랐다! 또 수업에 늦을 수는 없었다. 너무 부끄러울 것이었다! 그래서 나는 최대한 빨리 샤워를 하고 부리나케 옷을 입고 가방을 움켜잡고서는 버스 정류장으로 달렸다. 내가 막 도착했을 때 버스는 떠나고 있었다. 나는 "제발 저 좀 태워주세요!"하고 소리쳤다. 놀랍게도 버스가 멈췄다. 나는 버스를 타고 앉았다. 내 걱정은 끝이 났다.

8

M Are you going to Jen's birthday party?

W Of course! It would hurt her feelings if I didn't.

M Yeah, that's true. Can I get directions to Jack's house?

W Sure, I'll email them to you. You know the party is Tuesday, right?

M Yeah, I read that on the invitation. Do you know if there will be food?

W Yes. The plan is to eat hamburgers and play games.

M That sounds like fun. I'd better call Jen tonight and tell her I'm attending.

W Please do. They asked everyone to RSVP by Sunday.

남 너 Jen의 생일 파티에 갈 거야?

여 당연하지! 안 가면 그 애의 마음이 상할 텐데.

남 그래, 맞다. Jack네 집에 가는 길 좀 알려줄래?

여 그래, 이메일로 보내 줄게. 파티가 화요일인 거 알지?

남 응, 초대장에서 읽었어. 음식이 있을 건지 알아?

여 응, 계획은 햄버거를 먹고 게임을 하는 거야.

남 재미있겠다. 오늘 밤에 Jen한테 전화해서 내가 간다고 말해야겠어.

여 그래, 일요일까지 모두에게 회신을 달라고 했어.

UNIT VI DO YOU REMEMBER?

✿ Check Up

01 b   **02** 1.T 2.T 3.F

03 A John, <u>have you forgotten</u> your lunch again?

   B <u>I can't remember</u> if I brought it to school or not.

   A Maybe you left it at your house.

   B Probably so. It must have <u>slipped my mind</u>.

Check Up Scripts

01

W a. The boy and girl are watching a movie.

   b. The boy and girl are watching a sunset.

   c. The boy and girl are studying together.

여 a. 소년과 소녀가 영화를 보고 있다.

   b. 소년과 소녀가 해 지는 것을 바라보고 있다.

   c. 소년과 소녀가 함께 공부를 하고 있다.

Vocabulary	sunset 일몰

02

M Do you remember our first vacation?

W Of course. I'll never forget it.

M It was so exciting to go to the beach.

W I know. You'd never seen the ocean before.

M If only we could go back!

남 너 우리 첫 방학 기억해?

여 당연하지. 절대 잊을 수 없어.

남 바닷가에 간 건 너무 신났지.

여 알아. 넌 그 전에 바다를 본 적이 한 번도 없었지.

남 다시 돌아갈 수만 있다면!

Vocabulary	ocean 바다

03

A John, have you forgotten your lunch again?

B I can't remember if I brought it to school or not.

A Maybe you left it at your house.

B Probably so. It must have slipped my mind.

A John. 너 또 점심 잊어버렸니?

B 학교에 가져왔는지 아닌지 기억이 안 나.

A 어쩌면 집에 놓고 왔는지도 모르지.

B 아마 그랬을 거야. 깜박했나 봐.

Vocabulary	probably 아마도 slip one's mind 깜박 잊어버리다

Actual Test

1 ⑤ 2 ② 3 ③ 4 ⑤ 5 ⑤ 6 ③ 7 ① 8 ① | p.38

M <u>Do you remember</u> your first day of school?

W Of course I remember. I was <u>so nervous</u>!

남 너 학교 첫 날 기억나?

여 당연히 기억나지. 정말 긴장됐었어!

M Me too. <u>After all</u>, it was such a new experience.	남 나도야. 그러고 보면 정말 새로운 경험이었지.
W I <u>remember that</u> you forgot your coat, so I lent you mine.	여 네가 코트를 잊어버려서 내 걸 빌려줬던 게 기억나.
M I <u>forgot about that</u>. What a great memory!	남 난 그건 잊었는데. 대단한 기억력이다!
W Yes. That was when we first became friends.	여 응. 그때가 우리가 처음으로 친구가 되었던 때였어.

Vocabulary	experience 경험 lend 빌려주다 memory 기억력

2

W <u>Do you remember</u> what it was like to be a teenager?	여 십대라는 게 어떤 거였는지 기억나?
M Yeah. I don't want to <u>go through</u> that again.	남 응. 난 그때를 다시 겪고 싶지 않아.
W Whatever do you mean?	여 그게 무슨 뜻이니?
M I got <u>picked on</u> a lot in those days.	남 난 당시에 괴롭힘을 많이 당했어.
W You mean, by <u>bullies</u>?	여 약한 애들을 괴롭히는 애들한테 말이야?
M Yeah, they made fun of me <u>all the time</u>.	남 그래, 그 애들이 나를 항상 놀렸어.
W I'm sorry to hear that. Aren't you glad it's <u>in the past</u>?	여 그 말을 들으니 안됐다. 지나간 일이라서 기쁘지 않아?

Vocabulary	teenager 십대 go through ~을 겪다 pick on ~을 괴롭히다 bully 약자를 괴롭히는 사람
	all the time 항상 past 과거 present 현재

3

W Dear Parents,

I hope this letter finds you and your children well. I thank you <u>for attending</u> the school meeting last Friday afternoon. I just wanted to <u>remind everyone of</u> the big event that is coming next week. <u>Do you remember</u>? It's the Spring Festival, and everyone is invited! We are also <u>looking for</u> volunteers to sell food and work <u>on the games</u>. Please let me know if you are interested in <u>making the effort</u>.

Sincerely,
Principal Victoria

여 친애하는 학부모님들께

부모님과 자녀분들 모두 평안하시기를 바랍니다. 지난 금요일 오후에 있었던 학교 모임에 참석해 주셔서 감사합니다. 저는 단지 다음 주에 있을 중요한 행사에 대해서 모든 분들께 상기시켜 드리고자 합니다. 기억하십니까? 봄 축제입니다. 그리고 모든 분들을 초대합니다! 저희는 또한 음식을 팔고 게임에서 수고해 주실 자원봉사자들을 찾고 있습니다. 수고하시는 데 관심이 있으시면 저에게 알려 주십시오.

교장 Victoria

Vocabulary	remind A of B A에게 B를 상기시키다 invite 초대하다 volunteer 자원봉사자 effort 노력, 수고
	complain 불평하다 compliment 칭찬하다 announce 발표하다 apologize 사과하다

4

[The telephone rings.]

W Hey, Jack. <u>Have you forgotten about</u> our

[전화벨 소리]

여 이봐. Jack. 우리 운동에 대해서 잊어버렸어?

workout?

M You know I forget things <u>once in a while</u>. Where is the gym again?

여 내가 가끔 뭘 잊어버리는 거 알잖아. 체육관이 어디라고?

W Start at the science building and <u>turn right onto</u> University Way.

여 과학관에서 출발해서 University Way로 우회전해.

M OK. And what then?

남 알았어. 그 다음에는?

W Take the <u>first left</u> and drive past the baseball fields.

여 첫 번째 길에서 좌회전하고 야구장을 지나서 운전해.

M And then?

남 그리고?

W Turn left again at the next intersection. The gym will be the <u>first building on the right</u>.

여 다음 교차로에서 다시 좌회전해. 체육관은 오른쪽에 있는 첫 번째 건물일 거야.

M Thanks, I'll be there in a minute.

남 고마워. 곧 갈게.

Vocabulary	once in a while 가끔씩 gym 체육관 past ~을 지나서 intersection 교차로

5

M What was the <u>name of the movie</u> we saw last week?

남 우리가 지난주에 본 영화 제목이 뭐였지?

W <u>Have you forgotten already</u>? It was called *Law Man*.

여 벌써 잊어버렸어? 「Law Man」이었잖아.

M Oh, right. Now I <u>remember</u>. It was a Western, right?

남 오, 맞다. 이제 기억나. 서부영화였지?

W Yeah. It was about a man's attempt to save his town from outlaws.

여 그래. 어떤 남자가 무법자들로부터 마을을 구하려고 하는 내용이었잖아.

M Of course! <u>The action scenes</u> were really amazing.

남 그렇지! 액션 장면이 정말 굉장했어.

W Yes, but <u>in the end</u>, the cowboy defeated the bad guys and saved the day.

여 맞아. 하지만 마지막에는 카우보이가 악당들을 물리치고 승리했지.

Vocabulary	law 법 Western 서부영화 attempt 시도 save 구하다 outlaw 무법자 amazing 굉장한 in the end 마지막에 defeat 물리치다 save the day 겨우 승리하다, 궁지를 벗어나다

6

M Do you know what time it is? <u>It's time once again</u> for the citywide hot dog eating contest, held every year! Last year's winner ate <u>nearly 200</u> hot dogs! If you think you can <u>handle the challenge</u>, call us today at 555-1234 to enter the contest. The event begins at <u>12:00</u> in the City High School gym, but all eaters in the contest should <u>show up</u> an hour early.

남 지금이 무슨 때인지 아시나요? 매년 열리는, 전 도시의 핫도그 먹기 대회가 다시 한 번 돌아온 때입니다! 지난해의 우승자는 200개에 가까운 핫도그를 먹었죠! 당신이 도전을 감당할 수 있다고 생각하신다면 오늘 555-1234로 전화 주셔서 대회에 참가하세요. 행사는 12시 정각에 City 고등학교 체육관에서 시작되지만 모든 대회 참가자들은 한 시간 일찍 나타나야 합니다.

Vocabulary	citywide 전 도시의 contest 대회 handle 감당하다 challenge 도전 show up 나타나다

7

W I remember when I was <u>your</u> <u>age</u>, Danny.

M Really? What was <u>your</u> <u>childhood</u> <u>like</u>?

W Well, 30 years ago, we didn't have any of these <u>fancy</u> <u>toys</u> that you have now.

M What did you <u>do</u> for <u>fun</u>?

W We played outside all day, and we <u>listened</u> to the <u>radio</u> at night.

M You didn't have TV <u>back</u> <u>then</u>?

W Oh no, it was still new then, and much too expensive.

Vocabulary	childhood 어린 시절　fancy 멋진, 화려한

여 내가 네 나이였을 때가 기억난다. Danny.

남 정말요? 엄마 어린 시절은 어땠는데요?

여 음. 30년 전에 우리는 네가 지금 갖고 있는 이런 멋진 장난감은 하나도 없었지.

남 그럼 뭘 하면서 놀았어요?

여 하루 종일 밖에서 놀았어. 그리고 밤에는 라디오를 들었지.

남 그때는 TV가 없었어요?

여 오, 없었어. 그때만 해도 그건 새로운 것이었고 너무 비쌌단다.

8

M I'll <u>never</u> <u>forget</u> the first time my dad took me to a baseball game. I was <u>so</u> <u>excited</u>. I can still hear the <u>crowd</u> <u>cheering</u>. I can still smell the popcorn and the hot dogs. My dad bought me a new <u>baseball</u> <u>glove</u> just for that game. After the game, we even got the players' autographs. It was <u>the</u> <u>best</u> <u>day</u> of my life.

Vocabulary	crowd 관중　cheer 응원하다　smell 냄새를 맡다　autograph (유명인의) 사인

남 나는 아빠가 나를 야구장에 처음 데려간 때를 잊지 못할 것이다. 나는 정말 신이 났다. 난 아직도 관중들의 함성 소리를 들을 수 있다. 아직도 팝콘과 핫도그 냄새를 떠올릴 수 있다. 아빠는 그 경기만을 위한 새 야구 글러브를 사주셨다. 경기가 끝나고 나서 우리는 심지어 선수들의 사인도 받았다. 그날은 내 인생 최고의 날이었다.

UNIT VII ARE YOU SURE?

Check Up
p.43

01 c

02

	Frogs	Toads
Have rough, dry skin		✓
Always live near water	✓	
Have wet, smooth skin	✓	

03 A Did you know dogs and cats have feelings, just like people?

B <u>Are you sure</u> about that? I've always been told that they don't.

A <u>I'm confident</u> of it. My cat shows her feelings all the time.

B <u>I'm not sure</u>, but I think they feel things differently than people.

01

M	I love coming to the library.	남	난 도서관에 오는 게 너무 좋아.
W	I know. I'm come here all the time to read.	여	알아. 나도 (책을) 읽으러 항상 여기 와.
M	Have you seen this book? It's my favorite.	남	이 책 본 적 있어? 내가 제일 좋아하는 거야.
W	I've never read that one. Mind if I borrow it?	여	그건 안 읽어봤어. 내가 빌려가도 될까?
M	Sure, take a look at it. You might want to check it out.	남	그럼, 한번 봐봐. 대출하고 싶어질 거야.

> **Vocabulary**　check out ～을 대출하다

02

W	Did you know frogs are different from toads?	여	개구리가 두꺼비랑 다르다는 거 알고 있었어?
M	Are you sure about that?	남	그게 정말이야?
W	Of course. Frogs always live near water, and they have wet skin that's smooth.	여	그럼. 개구리는 물 근처에 살고 매끄러운 축축한 피부를 가졌어.
M	How is that different from a toad?	남	그게 두꺼비랑 어떻게 다른데?
W	A toad can live in dry places, and its skin is very rough.	여	두꺼비는 건조한 땅에서도 살 수 있고 피부가 아주 거칠어.

> **Vocabulary**　frog 개구리　toad 두꺼비　smooth 매끄러운　rough 거친

03

A	Did you know dogs and cats have feelings, just like people?	A	개와 고양이가 사람처럼 감정이 있다는 거 알고 있었어?
B	Are you sure about that? I've always been told that they don't.	B	그게 정말이야? 난 그렇지 않다고 항상 들어왔는데.
A	I'm confident of it. My cat shows her feelings all the time.	A	확실해. 내 고양이는 항상 감정을 나타내 보여.
B	I'm not sure, but I think they feel things differently than people.	B	난 잘 모르겠다. 하지만 그들이 사람과는 다른 방식으로 감정을 느낀다고 생각해.

> **Vocabulary**　confident 확신하는

Actual Test　　1 ⑤　2 ③　3 ①　4 ③　5 ⑤　6 ③　7 ④　8 ②　　| p.44

W	Are you ready to <u>check</u> <u>out</u>, sir?	여	대출할 준비가 되셨나요?
M	Yes, ma'am. I have <u>three</u> <u>books</u> here.	남	네. 여기 책 세 권이 있어요.

W OK. Just let me scan them into the computer.

M When should I return them?

W They are due back in exactly two weeks.

M Thanks, I'll probably return them a little early.

여 알겠습니다. 제가 그것들의 정보를 읽어서 컴퓨터에 입력할게요.

남 언제 반납해야 하죠?

여 정확히 2주 후가 반납 예정일입니다.

남 감사합니다. 아마 좀 더 일찍 반납할 것 같아요.

Vocabulary	check out ~을 대출하다 scan 정보를 읽다 return 반납하다 due 예정된

M Attention, all passengers. We regret to tell you that there is still some ice on the runway. The crew is working hard to clear it up. I'm not sure when we'll be able to take off, but I'm confident that it will be soon. Until then, we will be experiencing a slight delay. We thank you for your patience.

남 승객 여러분께 알립니다. 활주로에 아직도 약간의 얼음이 있다는 것을 알려드리게 되어 죄송합니다. 승무원들은 그것을 제거하기 위해 열심히 노력하고 있습니다. 언제 이륙할 수 있을지 확실치 않지만 곧 그렇게 될 것이라고 확신합니다. 그때까지 약간의 지연이 있을 것입니다. 여러분의 양해에 감사드립니다.

Vocabulary	passenger 승객 regret to ~하게 되어 유감이다 runway 활주로 crew 승무원 clear up ~을 제거하다 take off 이륙하다 experience 경험하다 delay 지연

W Hi, Mr. Robinson. I need to speak with you about my essay.

M Sure. What seems to be the problem?

W Well, I'm going on vacation this week.

M You know the essay is due on Wednesday, right?

W I know. But since I'll be out of town…

M You want an extension on the deadline.

W If you're willing to give me one, yes.

M I'll let you turn it in two days past the deadline. But no later.

W I'm pretty sure I can do that. Thanks!

여 안녕하세요. Robinson 선생님. 제 에세이에 대해서 말씀 좀 나누고 싶은데요.

남 그래. 문제가 뭔데 그러니?

여 음. 제가 이번 주에 놀러 가서요.

남 에세이가 수요일까지인 거 알고 있지?

여 알아요. 그런데 제가 도시 밖으로 나갈 거라서…

남 제출 기한을 연장해달라는 말이구나.

여 그래 주실 마음이 있으시다면요.

남 마감일보다 이틀 후에 제출하도록 해주마. 하지만 더 늦으면 안 된다.

여 그건 분명히 할 수 있어요. 감사합니다!

Vocabulary	due 예정인 extension 연장 deadline 마감일, 마감 시간 be willing to 기꺼이 ~하다 past ~을 지나서

4

M Are you ready to go to the party?

W Not yet. I can't find my necklace.

M Are you serious? We're already late.

W As soon as I find it, we'll go.

M Where do you think it might be?

남 파티에 갈 준비 됐어?

여 아직. 목걸이를 찾을 수가 없네.

남 정말이야? 우리 벌써 늦었는데.

여 그걸 찾는 대로 갈 거야.

남 어디에 있을 것 같아?

W Well, I picked it up off the <u>night table</u>.

M OK. Is it on the bed next to the table?

W No, I looked there already. After the bed, I went <u>to the closet</u> to get a sweater.

M What about when you were <u>at the dresser</u>?

W No, I didn't take it off then.

M I also saw you over <u>by the window</u>.

W That must be where I left it!

여 음, 내가 침실 탁자에서 그걸 집어 들었어.

남 좋아. 탁자 옆에 있는 침대에 있어?

여 아니야. 거긴 벌써 봤지. 침대 다음에는 스웨터를 가지러 옷장에 갔었어.

남 서랍장에 있었을 때는 어때?

여 아니야, 거기에 내려놓지 않았어.

남 네가 창문 옆에 있는 것도 봤는데.

여 내가 거기에 그걸 둔게 분명해.

| Vocabulary | necklace 목걸이   night table 침실용 탁자   closet 벽장, 옷장   dresser 서랍장 |

5

W Thank you for visiting City Zoo. We hope you enjoy <u>your</u> visit. We'd like to remind you <u>not</u> to <u>approach</u> the cages too closely. This may <u>disturb the animals</u>. Also, we'd like to remind you of our <u>new exhibit</u>. For a short period, we have two new gorillas <u>on display</u>. Hurry and see them now, because they won't be here <u>for long</u>. We're <u>confident</u> you'll love it!

여 시립 동물원을 찾아 주셔서 감사합니다. 여러분의 방문을 즐기시기 바랍니다. 우리에 너무 가까이 다가가지 말 것을 상기시켜 드립니다. 이것은 동물들을 방해할 수 있습니다. 또한 저희의 새로운 전시에 대해서도 상기시켜 드리고자 합니다. 짧은 기간 동안 저희는 새로운 고릴라 두 마리를 보여드리고 있습니다. 그들이 여기 오래 있지 않을 것이니 서둘러서 지금 그들을 보십시오. 여러분께서 좋아하실 것이라고 확신합니다!

| Vocabulary | approach 다가가다   cage 우리   disturb 방해하다   exhibit 전시   period 기간   display 전시
confident 확신하는 |

6

M Did you <u>hear about</u> the foreign language classes?

W Yeah, the community college <u>offers them</u> at night.

M Do you know the <u>days</u> <u>and times</u> of the classes?

W Well, there's <u>Spanish</u> at 6:00 on <u>Monday</u>.

M What about French?

W <u>French class</u> is at 7:00 on Tuesday.

M Are you <u>sure about that</u>? I heard French is on Wednesday.

W No, Wednesday is <u>Japanese</u> at <u>6:00</u>.

M Oh, you're right. Do you think you'll <u>take a class</u>?

W I'm not sure <u>at the moment</u>. Either English, at 8:00 on Thursdays, or German, at 6:00 on Fridays.

남 외국어 강의에 대해서 들었어?

여 응. 지역 대학에서 야간 강의를 제공한다며.

남 강의 날짜하고 시간 알아?

여 음, 월요일 6시에 스페인어가 있어.

남 프랑스어는?

여 프랑스어는 화요일 7시에 있어.

남 그거 확실해? 난 프랑스어가 수요일이라고 들었는데.

여 아니야, 수요일은 6시에 일본어가 있어.

남 아, 네 말이 맞다. 너 수업 들을 거라고 생각하니?

여 지금으로서는 잘 모르겠어. 목요일 8시에 하는 영어 아니면 금요일 6시에 하는 독일어를 들을까 해.

7

W Mary arrives in Spain for vacation. She is so excited to finally be there! Unfortunately, she didn't bring much money with her, and now she needs a place to stay for the night. It is getting dark, so the situation is urgent. She finds a small hostel and walks up to the desk. She pulls all the money out of her pocket and shows it to the desk clerk. In this situation, what is Mary likely to say?

여 Mary는 휴가를 보내려고 스페인에 도착합니다. 그녀는 마침내 그곳에 있게 되어 너무 신납니다! 안타깝게도 그녀는 돈을 그다지 많이 가져오지 않았고 지금 밤에 묵을 곳이 필요합니다. 어두워지고 있어서 상황이 급박하다. 그녀는 작은 호스텔을 발견하고 데스크로 걸어갑니다. 그녀는 주머니에 있는 돈을 모두 꺼내고 그것을 데스크 직원에게 보여줍니다. 이 상황에서 Mary는 뭐라고 말하겠습니까?

8

① **M** Would you like to go to the park with me?

   W I wish I could, but I'm very busy at the moment.

② **M** Do you think you passed the chemistry test?

   W No, I think I left my homework on the bus.

③ **M** When does the next bus arrive?

   W The buses come in 10-minute intervals.

④ **M** Let's see if there's anything on TV.

   W Are you serious? We're supposed to be studying.

⑤ **M** Are you sure that Matt will meet us there?

   W Yes, he said to meet him at the restaurant.

① **남** 나랑 같이 공원에 갈래?

   여 그럴 수 있으면 좋겠는데 지금은 무척 바빠.

② **남** 너 화학 시험 통과한 거 같아?

   여 아니, 숙제를 버스에 놓고 내린 것 같아.

③ **남** 다음 버스는 언제 도착하지?

   여 버스는 10분 간격으로 와.

④ **남** TV에서 뭐하는지 보자.

   여 진심이야? 우린 공부를 하고 있어야 하잖아.

⑤ **남** Matt이 거기서 우리를 만날 것이 확실해?

   여 응, 그가 그 식당에서 만나자고 했어.

UNIT VIII GUESS WHAT!

Check Up

01 b **02** b

03 A Guess what happened to Carl today at school?

B I heard he got into a fight. He must be in big trouble now.

A You got that right. My guess is he'll be kicked out of school.

B I bet you're right. Poor Carl!

Check Up Scripts

01

a. M Guess what? We're going out to dinner.

W Great! Where do you want to go?

b. M This food is great. I haven't eaten all day.

W Wow. You must be really hungry.

c. M What would you like to order, sir?

W Um, I guess I'll have the spaghetti.

a. 남 있잖아? 우리 저녁 먹으러 나갈 거야.

여 좋아! 어디로 가고 싶어?

b. 남 이 음식 정말 맛있다. 난 하루 종일 먹지 못했어.

여 와. 너 정말 배고프겠구나.

c. 남 무엇을 주문하시겠습니까, 손님?

여 음, 스파게티로 할까 해요.

Vocabulary	order 주문하다

02

W I tried baking a cake today, but it didn't turn out very well. I think I put too much flour in it. It didn't rise at all in the oven. When it came out, it was all flat. And it tasted terrible! I guess I need a little more practice.

여 나는 오늘 케이크를 구워 보았는데 썩 잘 되지 않았다. 밀가루를 너무 많이 넣은 것 같다. 케이크가 오븐에서 전혀 부풀어오르질 않았다. 꺼냈을 때 그것은 온통 납작했다. 그리고 맛이 형편없었다! 난 좀 더 연습이 필요한 것 같다.

Vocabulary	try -ing ~해보다 turn out 결과가 ~하게 되다 flour 밀가루 flat 납작한 taste ~한 맛이 나다 practice 연습

03

A Guess what happened to Carl today at school?

B I heard he got into a fight. He must be in big trouble now.

A You got that right. My guess is he'll be kicked out of school.

B I bet you're right. Poor Carl!

A 오늘 학교에서 Carl에게 무슨 일이 있었는지 알아?

B 싸움에 말려들었다고 들었어. 지금쯤 큰 곤경에 처해 있겠다.

A 맞아. 내 생각에 그는 퇴학당할 것 같아.

B 틀림없어. 불쌍한 Carl!

Vocabulary	happen 일어나다 fight 싸움 trouble 곤경 be kicked out of school 퇴학당하다

1

W How is your science project going?

M I'm making a lot of progress. In fact, I'm almost finished.

W You must be working really hard then.

M Oh, I am. I'm up late every night working on it.

W Well, I hope you get a good grade for your work.

M Thanks, and good luck on your project as well.

여	과학 프로젝트 어떻게 되어 가?
남	많이 진전되고 있어. 사실 난 거의 끝나가.
여	그럼 정말 열심히 하고 있나 보구나.
남	어, 그래. 매일 밤 늦게까지 그것에 매달리고 있어.
여	음, 네 작업에 대해서 좋은 성적을 받으면 좋겠다.
남	고마워, 그리고 네 프로젝트도 잘 되길 바랄게.

| Vocabulary | make progress 진전을 이루다   in fact 사실은   work on ~에 공을 들이다   grade 성적   as well ~도 역시 |

2

M ① The girl is trying to walk her dog.
② The boy is mixing a recipe in a bowl.
③ The boy is sleeping at his school desk.
④ The girl is jogging in the park.
⑤ The girl is carrying her backpack to school.

남	① 소녀가 개를 산책시키려 하고 있다.
	② 소년이 그릇에 요리 재료를 섞고 있다.
	③ 소년이 학교 책상에서 자고 있다.
	④ 소녀가 공원에서 조깅을 하고 있다.
	⑤ 소녀가 가방을 메고 학교에 가고 있다.

| Vocabulary | walk 산책시키다   mix 섞다   recipe 조리법, 요리 재료   backpack 뒤로 메는 가방 |

3

M Do you know what you'd like to eat, ma'am?

W Yes, I'll have the chef's salad to start.

M Excellent choice. And what else?

W Also, a bowl of vegetable soup. Is it made from fresh vegetables?

M Only the freshest, ma'am. Will that be all?

W You know what? I'll have a club sandwich, too.

M OK. Your food should be ready shortly.

남	무엇을 드시고 싶으신지 결정하셨나요?
여	네, 우선 주방장 추천 샐러드를 먹을게요.
남	탁월한 선택이십니다. 다른 것은요?
여	또, 야채 수프 한 그릇 주세요. 신선한 야채로 만들어지나요?
남	가장 신선한 것들로만요. 그게 전부입니까?
여	있잖아요? 클럽 샌드위치도 먹을게요.
남	알겠습니다. 주문하신 음식이 곧 준비될 것입니다.

| Vocabulary | chef 주방장   choice 선택   bowl 그릇   shortly 곧 |

4

M May I <u>have</u> <u>your</u> <u>attention</u>, please? Thank you all for coming to my <u>daughter's</u> <u>wedding</u>. It truly has been a wonderful day. It seems like just yesterday, my daughter was a little girl. And <u>suddenly</u>, she has become an adult. But I'm <u>confident</u> <u>that</u> she and her new husband will be happy for <u>many</u> <u>years</u> <u>to</u> <u>come</u>.

Question Which statement best describes the situation?

남 잠깐 주목해 주시겠습니까? 제 딸의 결혼식에 와주신 모든 분들께 감사를 드립니다. 정말 멋진 날입니다. 제 딸이 어린 소녀였을 때가 엊그제 같은데요. 이제 갑자기 그 애가 어른이 되었네요. 하지만 저는 그 애와 새로운 남편이 앞으로 오랫동안 행복할 것이라고 확신합니다.

질문 어떤 문장이 상황을 가장 잘 설명하는가?

Vocabulary	attention 주의, 주목 suddenly 갑자기 adult 성인, 어른 confident 확신하는

5

M I'm <u>worried</u> <u>about</u> my garden. I planted it weeks ago, but nothing is growing.

W These things <u>take</u> <u>time</u>. Plants grow <u>very</u> <u>gradually</u>.

M You're right. I guess I'm just <u>getting</u> <u>impatient</u>.

W Probably so. Are you watering them <u>regularly</u>?

M Yes. But they don't get <u>as</u> <u>much</u> sunlight as they could.

W <u>Try</u> <u>to</u> <u>increase</u> the amount of sun, and see <u>what</u> <u>happens</u>.

M OK. Thanks for the help, Pam.

남 정원에 대해서 걱정이 돼서. 일주일 전에 심었는데 아무것도 자라지 않고 있어.

여 이런 일은 시간이 걸려. 식물은 아주 천천히 자라.

남 네 말이 맞아. 내가 그냥 좀 초조해지고 있나 봐.

여 아마 그럴 거야. 규칙적으로 물을 주고 있니?

남 응. 하지만 받을 수 있는 만큼의 햇빛은 못 받고 있어.

여 햇빛의 양을 늘려보도록 해봐. 그리고 어떻게 되나 봐.

남 알겠어. 도움 줘서 고마워, Pam.

Vocabulary	plant 심다; 식물 grow 자라다 take time 시간이 걸리다 gradually 천천히, 점진적으로 impatient 초조한 water 물을 주다 regularly 규칙적으로 sunlight 햇빛, 일광 increase 늘리다

6

M OK, class, please <u>listen</u> <u>up</u>. Today in health class we will be <u>talking</u> <u>about</u> nutrition. Basically, your body uses food like a car uses <u>fuel</u>. It takes all the vitamins and minerals <u>in</u> <u>the</u> <u>food</u> and rapidly converts them into energy. Without these things, your body would quickly <u>stop</u> <u>working</u>, just like a car that is <u>out</u> <u>of</u> <u>gas</u>. This is why you can <u>die</u> <u>of</u> <u>hunger</u>. As you decrease your food, your body produces less and <u>less</u> <u>energy</u>.

남 좋아요, 여러분, 잘 들으세요. 오늘 보건 수업에서는 영양에 대해 이야기할 거예요. 기본적으로 여러분의 몸은 자동차가 연료를 사용하듯이 음식을 사용해요. 그것은 음식에서 모든 비타민과 미네랄을 취해서 그것들을 빨리 에너지로 변환시키죠. 이런 것들이 없다면 여러분의 몸은 금방 작동을 멈출 거예요. 마치 자동차가 휘발유가 떨어지면 그런 것처럼 말이죠. 이것이 배고픔으로 죽을 수 있는 이유예요. 음식을 줄이면 여러분의 몸은 점점 더 적은 에너지를 생산하죠.

Vocabulary	Listen up. 잘 들어. nutrition 영양 basically 기본적으로 fuel 연료 mineral 미네랄, 광물 rapidly 빨리
	convert A into B A를 B로 변환시키다 gas 휘발유 die of ~으로 죽다 decrease 줄이다 produce 생산하다

7

[The telephone rings.]	[전화벨 소리]
M Hello?	남 여보세요?
W Hi, this is Carol. I'm calling for Mike.	여 안녕하세요, 저는 Carol인데요. Mike에게 전화했어요.
M Oh, I'm afraid Mike is out right now. Shall I take a message?	남 아. Mike는 지금 밖에 나갔는데. 남길 말이 있니?
W Can you tell Mike to meet me after school?	여 Mike에게 학교 끝나고 저를 만나달라고 말씀해 주시겠어요?
M Sure. Where should he meet you?	남 그럼. 어디서 만나야 하니?
W At the library. We planned to study together today.	여 도서관에서요. 같이 공부를 하려고 하거든요.
M OK. I'll let him know.	남 그래. 말해 줄게.
W Thanks, Mr. Weathers!	여 감사합니다. Weathers 씨!

Vocabulary	pleasure 즐거움, 기쁨

8

M You know what? I couldn't ask for a better job. Every day, my coworkers and I work hard to develop new medicines. Our goal is to make life easier for people. We work to reduce the amount of disease and sickness in the world. In that way, I always feel like I'm doing my part to make the world a better place.	남 그거 아세요? 전 더 나은 직업을 요구할 수가 없습니다. 매일 제 동료들과 저는 신약을 개발하기 위해서 열심히 일합니다. 우리의 목표는 사람들에게 삶을 더 쉽게 만드는 것입니다. 우리는 세계에 있는 질병과 질환의 양을 줄이려고 노력합니다. 그렇게 해서 저는 언제나 제가 세계를 더 나은 곳으로 만드는 데 제 역할을 하고 있다고 느낍니다.

Vocabulary	ask for ~을 요구하다 coworker 동료 develop 개발하다 medicine 약 goal 목표 amount 양
	disease / sickness 질병 do one's part 자신의 역할을 하다

UNIT IX YOU'RE SUPPOSED TO BE CAREFUL.

Check Up

p.55

01 b 02 1.F 2.T 3.F

03 A Grace, you're supposed to be doing your homework.

B Do I have to? I'd rather be watching television.

A You can watch TV later. Right now, make sure you finish that homework assignment. And be careful not to make any mistakes.

B OK, Dad. I will.

Check Up Scripts

01

M What does that road sign mean?

W The red and white sign?

M Yes, the triangle shaped sign.

W Oh, it means you're supposed to be careful, and watch out for other cars.

M Oh, I see.

남 저 도로 표지판은 무슨 뜻이야?

여 빨갛고 하얀 표지판 말이야?

남 응. 삼각형 모양의 표지판.

여 아, 그건 조심해야 한다는 거야. 다른 차들을 주의하고.

남 오, 알겠어.

| Vocabulary | road sign 도로 표지판   be supposed to ~하기로 되어 있다   careful 조심하는   watch out for ~을 조심하다 |

02

W Your cooking is the best I've had.

M Thank you. I do hope to be a chef one day.

W Well, you should have no problems.

M What did you think of my pasta dish?

W It was perfect. What's your secret?

M You must use just the right amount of seasoning.

여 네 요리는 내가 먹어본 것 중 최고야.

남 고마워. 언젠가 요리사가 되면 정말 좋겠어.

여 음, 넌 아무 문제 없을 거야.

남 내 파스타 요리 어땠어?

여 완벽했어. 비결이 뭐니?

남 양념을 적당량만큼만 넣어야 해.

| Vocabulary | chef 요리사, 주방장   dish 요리   amount 양   seasoning 양념 |

03

A Grace, you're supposed to be doing your homework.

B Do I have to? I'd rather be watching television.

A Right now, make sure you finish that homework assignment. And be careful not to make any mistakes.

B OK, Dad. I will.

A Grace. 너 숙제 하고 있어야 하잖니.

B 그래야 해요? 전 그보다 텔레비전을 보고 싶은데요.

A 지금 당장은 그 숙제를 반드시 끝내도록 해. 그리고 실수하지 않도록 조심하고.

B 네, 아빠. 그럴게요.

| Vocabulary | be supposed to ~하기로 되어 있다   I'd rather 차라리 ~하겠다   make sure 반드시 ~하다   assignment 과제   mistake 실수 |

1

W Excuse me, waiter?

M How can I help you, ma'am?

W I'm afraid there was a mistake with my food.

M Oh, I'm very sorry to hear that. What seems to be the problem?

W Well, my steak is overcooked. It's very dry and tough.

M I'd be happy to have the chef cook you another.

W That's fine. Just be careful not to overcook it again.

여 저기요, 웨이터?

남 부르셨습니까?

여 제 음식에 실수가 있었던 것 같네요.

남 오. 정말 죄송합니다. 문제가 무엇인가요?

여 음. 제 스테이크가 너무 익혀졌어요. 아주 뻣뻣하고 질겨요.

남 주방장에게 말해서 하나 더 요리하라고 말하겠습니다.

여 괜찮아요. 그냥 다음에 또 다시 너무 익히지 않도록 주의해 주세요.

Vocabulary	mistake 실수 overcook 너무 익히다 tough 질긴 chef 주방장

2

W Mike, will you help me in the kitchen?

M Sure, I'm very handy in the kitchen. What would you like me to do?

W Chop some fresh vegetables for dinner, please.

M No problem. Would you like me to cook them?

W Yes, if you don't mind. I was going to steam them.

M Oh, I love steamed vegetables. I make them at home all the time.

W Great. Do you think you'll need any help?

여 Mike. 부엌에서 나 좀 도와줄래?

남 그럼. 나 부엌에서 아주 쓸 만해. 내가 뭘 하면 좋겠어?

여 저녁에 먹을 신선한 야채 좀 썰어줘.

남 문제 없어. 그것들을 요리할까?

여 괜찮다면 그래 줘. 찌려고 하고 있었어.

남 오, 나 찐 야채 정말 좋아해. 집에서 항상 그렇게 해 먹어.

여 잘 됐다. 도움이 필요할 것 같니?

Vocabulary	handy 유용한 chop (음식 재료를 토막으로) 썰다 steam 찌다 all the time 항상

3

M OK, everyone. First we're going to mix the butter, flour, and eggs in one bowl. Stir that mixture until it all blends together. When it thickens, it's ready to go into the cake pan. Pour the mixture into the pan and set the oven for 350 degrees. Bake for about 30

남 좋아요, 여러분. 우선 그릇 하나에다가 버터, 밀가루, 계란을 섞을게요. 모두 잘 섞일 때까지 그 혼합물을 저으세요. 걸쭉해지면 케이크 팬에 넣을 준비가 된 거예요. 혼합물을 팬에 붓고 오븐을 350도로 맞추세요. 약 30분 동안 구우세요. 요리가 잘 되고 있는지 확인하기 위해서 이따금씩 들여다 보셔야 해요. 주의를 기울이세요.

36

minutes. You have to check it <u>now</u> and <u>then</u>, to make sure it's cooking properly, so <u>pay</u> <u>close</u> <u>attention</u>.

| Vocabulary | mix 섞다   stir 휘젓다   mixture 혼합물   blend 섞이다   thicken 걸쭉해지다   pour 따르다, 붓다 |
| | degree 도   now and then 이따금씩   properly 제대로 |

4

M What are you doing this weekend, Bernice?

W I'm <u>spending</u> <u>time</u> <u>with</u> my parents.

M That sounds nice. Do you see them often?

W <u>Not</u> <u>as</u> <u>much</u> <u>as</u> I should. I always enjoy my visits, though.

M What do you like best about them?

W Well, I love my <u>mother's</u> <u>cooking</u>. Every time I visit, she roasts a duck.

M Mm, that <u>sounds</u> <u>delicious</u>.

W Oh, it is. Her roast duck is the best I've had.

Question What does the woman like most about visiting her parents?

남	이번 주말에 뭐 할 거야, Bernice?
여	부모님이랑 시간을 보낼 거야.
남	그거 좋네. 그분들을 자주 뵙니?
여	내가 해야 하는 만큼 많이는 아니야. 하지만 거기 가면 언제나 좋아.
남	가면 제일 좋은 게 뭐야?
여	음. 난 엄마 요리를 정말 좋아해. 내가 갈 때마다 엄마가 오리를 구워 주셔.
남	음. 그거 맛있겠다.
여	어. 그래. 엄마의 오리 구이는 내가 먹어본 것 중 최고야.
질문	여자가 부모님 댁을 방문하는 것에서 가장 좋아하는 것은 무엇인가?

| Vocabulary | visit 방문   roast 굽다   recipe 요리법 |

5

W For your birthday, I'm going to cook you a <u>special</u> <u>meal</u>.

M That sounds great! <u>Can</u> <u>I</u> <u>choose</u> anything I want?

W <u>Of</u> <u>course</u>! It's your birthday, after all.

M I think I want lobster tails. I <u>haven't</u> <u>had</u> <u>them</u> in a long time.

W OK. How do you like it prepared?

M You're <u>supposed</u> <u>to</u> <u>broil</u> them in the oven.

W And how does one <u>serve</u> <u>lobster</u> <u>tail</u>?

M Usually just with melted butter and <u>a</u> <u>slice</u> <u>of</u> <u>lemon</u>.

여	네 생일에 특별 요리를 하려고 해.
남	그거 좋은데! 내가 원하는 거 아무거나 골라도 돼?
여	당연하지! 당신 생일인데.
남	나는 바닷가재 꼬리를 먹고 싶어. 오랫동안 못 먹어봤거든.
여	알겠어. 어떻게 조리하기를 원해?
남	오븐에서 구워야 해.
여	그리고 어떻게 바닷가재 꼬리를 내면 되지?
남	보통은 녹인 버터랑 레몬 조각을 곁들여.

| Vocabulary | meal 식사   tail 꼬리   prepare 준비하다   broil 굽다   serve (음식을) 내다   melt 녹이다 |

M Barbecue has a long tradition in the United States. The first barbecue was made by poor people, who couldn't afford expensive meat. The meat that is used was once the cheapest available. For this reason, it was often tough. So in order to cook it, people had to slowly roast it over low heat for a long time. After that, it became tender and delicious, and easy to eat.

남 바비큐는 미국에서 오래된 전통을 갖고 있습니다. 최초의 바비큐는 비싼 고기를 살 여유가 없었던 가난한 사람들에 의해 만들어졌습니다. (바비큐에) 사용되는 고기는 구할 수 있는 가장 싼 것이었습니다. 이런 이유로 그것은 종종 질겼습니다. 그래서 그것을 요리하기 위해 사람들은 그것을 약한 불에 오랫동안 천천히 구워야 했습니다. 그러고 나면 그것은 부드럽고 맛있어졌고 먹기 쉬워졌습니다.

Vocabulary	barbecue 바비큐　tradition 전통　afford ~할 여유가 있다　once 한때　available 구할 수 있는
	tough 질긴　roast 굽다　tender 부드러운

M I've always loved making things with my hands. It isn't always easy to build the things I do, but it is always fun. I make all kinds of things. Chairs, tables, cabinets—no job is too big for me. The most important thing to remember is to be careful. My father, who taught me to work with wood, always said, "Measure twice, cut once." In other words, you must be careful to measure correctly. This way, you never make a mistake, and the job goes faster.

남 저는 언제나 손으로 물건을 만드는 일을 좋아했습니다. 제가 만드는 것들을 만들기가 언제나 쉽지만은 않지만 그것은 항상 즐겁습니다. 저는 온갖 것들을 만듭니다. 의자, 탁자, 수납장 등. 어떤 일도 저에겐 벅차지 않습니다. 기억해야 할 가장 중요한 것은 주의하는 것입니다. 저에게 목공 일을 가르쳐주신 아버지는 늘 말씀하셨습니다. "두 번 재단하고 한 번 잘라라." 다시 말해 정확히 재단하기 위해서는 신중해야 한다는 것이죠. 이런 식으로 하면 절대 실수를 하지 않고 그러면 작업은 빨라집니다.

Vocabulary	cabinet 수납장　careful 주의하는, 신중한　measure 재단하다　in other words 다시 말해　correctly 정확히

W Who is your favorite painter, Miguel?

M I like a lot of painters. But I think Monet is my favorite.

W Which of his paintings do you like the best?

M I can't remember the name of it. It features a bridge, though.

W Oh yes, I know that one. A bridge over a pond, right?

M Yes, a small pond with flowers floating in it.

W That is certainly a lovely painting.

M I'd love to see it. I hear it's in a museum in New York.

W Then we absolutely must go there someday!

여 네가 제일 좋아하는 화가는 누구야, Miguel?

남 나는 많은 화가를 좋아해. 하지만 Monet가 내가 제일 좋아하는 화가인 것 같아.

여 그의 그림 중 어떤 것이 제일 좋은데?

남 제목은 기억이 안 나. 하지만 다리가 있는 게 특징이야.

여 아, 그래. 나 그거 알아. 연못에 다리가 있는 거 맞지?

남 그래, 작은 연못에 꽃잎이 떠다니고 있지.

여 그거 확실히 예쁜 그림이지.

남 그걸 보고 싶어. 뉴욕에 있는 박물관에 있다고 하던데.

여 그러면 우리 언젠가 거기 꼭 가야겠다!

UNIT X I'LL KEEP THAT IN MIND.

✪ Check Up

p.61

01 b

02

	Soccer	Basketball
More exciting		✓
Very challenging	✓	
More popular	✓	

03 **A** I've decided to study literature when I go to university.

    B I hope you can find a job after you graduate. It might be difficult.

    A Well, I'll keep that in mind. But I'm sure I'll be OK.

    B All right. I wish you all the best in the future.

Check Up Scripts

01

M **a.** The students are beginning college.	남 **a.** 학생들이 대학에 입학하고 있다.
b. The students are graduating.	**b.** 학생들이 졸업하고 있다.
c. The students talk with their teachers.	**c.** 학생들이 선생님들과 이야기를 하고 있다.

02

W I've decided to quit the basketball team.	여 나 농구 팀 그만두기로 결심했어.
M Why? I thought you loved basketball.	남 왜? 난 네가 농구를 정말 좋아하는 줄 알았는데.
W I like soccer better. It's more challenging.	여 난 축구가 더 좋아. 더 많은 노력을 필요로 하거든.
M True, but basketball is more exciting.	남 사실이야. 하지만 농구가 더 재미있지.
W You're right. But soccer is more popular around the world.	여 맞아. 하지만 축구는 전 세계에서 더 인기가 있어.
M You're right about that. Well, I hope you enjoy it.	남 그건 네 말이 맞다. 음, 네가 그걸 즐기길 바랄게.

A I've decided to study literature when I go to university.

B I hope you can find a job after you graduate. It might be difficult.

A Well, I'll keep that in mind. But I'm sure I'll be OK.

B All right. I wish you all the best in the future.

A 나는 대학에서 문학을 공부하기로 결심했어.

B 졸업 후에 일자리를 찾을 수 있기를 바라. 어려울 수도 있어.

A 음. 그걸 염두에 둘게. 하지만 난 괜찮을 거라고 확신해.

B 좋아. 네 장래에 행운을 빌게.

Vocabulary	literature 문학　　keep ~ in mind ~을 염두에 두다

Actual Test

1 ②　2 ③　3 ⑤　4 ②　5 ②　6 ②　7 ③　8 ⑤　　| p.62

W So, are you going to camp this summer?

M No, I'm visiting my cousin in Los Angeles.

W That's so exciting. What will you do there?

M I want to take a tour of Hollywood, for sure.

W Maybe you'll see some famous movie stars.

M I hope so! That would be great!

W Well, best of luck on your trip. Have fun!

M Thanks. I can't wait!

여 그래. 너 이번 여름에 캠프에 갈 거야?

남 아니, 난 LA에 사는 사촌 집에 갈 거야.

여 그거 정말 신난다. 거기서 뭘 할 거야?

남 헐리우드 투어는 꼭 하고 싶어.

여 어쩌면 유명한 영화배우들을 볼지도 모르겠다.

남 그러길 바라! 그럼 정말 좋을 거야!

여 음. 네 여행에 행운을 빌게. 재미있게 지내!

남 고마워. 너무 기다려져!

Vocabulary	cousin 사촌　　take a tour of ~을 둘러보다, 투어를 하다　　for sure 물론, 반드시

M Mrs. Martin, do you mind if we talk?

W Sure. How can I help you, Eric?

M Well, I feel like I'm not doing well in your class.

W I've noticed this. Is there any way I can help?

M I don't know. I'm starting to think it's just too difficult.

W I understand. Maybe you should take better notes in class.

M That's a good idea. I think I've made up my mind to do that.

남 Martin 선생님, 잠깐 말씀 나눌 수 있을까요?

여 그럼. 무슨 일이야, Eric?

남 저, 제가 선생님 수업에서 잘 못 하고 있는 것 같아서요.

여 나도 눈치 챘어. 내가 도울 수 있는 방법이 있을까?

남 모르겠어요. 그냥 너무 어렵다고 생각하기 시작해서요.

여 이해해. 어쩌면 넌 수업시간에 필기를 더 잘 해야 할지 모르겠다.

남 그거 좋은 생각이에요. 전 그러기로 결심한 것 같아요.

W Good. With a little hard work, I know you'll do fine.

여 좋아. 좀 더 열심히 노력하면 넌 잘 할 거라는 걸 알고 있단다.

3

W OK, class, we will be talking about ancient cultures. Who can tell me the <u>differences between</u> Ancient Rome and Ancient Greece? For one thing, Rome was a larger state, with a great army. Greece, <u>on the other hand</u>, was a collection of small states. And they focused on the arts <u>more than war</u> and violence. You should be <u>taking notes</u>, by the way. I've <u>decided to</u> give a quiz on this later.

여 좋아요, 여러분. 고대 문화에 대해 이야기할 거예요. 고대 로마와 고대 그리스의 차이를 누가 말해줄 수 있나요? 한 가지로 로마는 더 큰 국가였고 강력한 군대가 있었어요. 반면 그리스는 작은 국가들의 모임이었죠. 그리고 그들은 전쟁과 폭력보다 예술에 더 집중했어요. 그건 그렇고, 여러분은 필기를 하셔야 할 거예요. 이것에 대해서 나중에 퀴즈를 보기로 했거든요.

4

① **W** This is the best computer game ever!

M I'm glad you like it! <u>Would you like to</u> buy it?

① **여** 이건 최고의 컴퓨터 게임이에요!

남 좋아하시니 기쁘네요! 구입하시겠어요?

② **M** I need a new computer to use at college.

W This model here is very <u>popular with students</u>.

② **남** 대학에서 쓸 새 컴퓨터가 필요해요.

여 여기 이 모델은 학생들에게 인기가 아주 많습니다.

③ **W** Can you direct me to the computer department?

M Of course. It's <u>down this way</u>, on the left.

③ **여** 컴퓨터 부서로 가는 길을 알려주시겠어요?

남 물론이죠. 이쪽으로 가시면 되고요, 왼쪽에 있습니다.

④ **M** I wish <u>I could afford</u> a new computer.

W Maybe you can get a <u>part-time</u> job and earn the money.

④ **남** 새 컴퓨터를 살 돈이 있었으면 좋겠어.

여 넌 아마 아르바이트를 얻어서 돈을 벌 수 있을 거야.

⑤ **W** I've <u>made up my mind</u> to buy this television.

M You made an <u>excellent choice</u>. It's one of our best.

⑤ **여** 이 텔레비전을 사기로 결심했어요.

남 탁월한 선택입니다. 저희 최고의 제품이죠.

M Dear Miss Green,

Thank you for being in our poetry contest. The judges really enjoyed reading your work. Unfortunately, you did not win. However, your writing shows a lot of talent for someone as young as you. As a result, we would like you to attend the awards ceremony. There, you can read your wonderful poetry to the audience. We hope you will attend, and we wish you all the best.

남 친애하는 Green 양.

저희 시 경연대회에 참가해 주셔서 감사합니다. 심사위원들은 귀하의 작품을 읽는 것을 정말 좋아했습니다. 안타깝게도 귀하는 우승을 하지 못했습니다. 하지만 귀하의 글은 귀하처럼 어린 사람으로서는 많은 재능을 보여줍니다. 그래서 저희는 귀하가 시상식에 참석해 주셨으면 합니다. 그곳에서 귀하는 청중에게 귀하의 훌륭한 시를 읽어줄 수 있습니다. 귀하가 참석하기를 바라며, 귀하의 앞날에 행운이 가득하기를 빕니다.

Vocabulary	contest 경연대회 judge 심사위원 unfortunately 안타깝게도 talent 재능 attend 참석하다
	awards ceremony 시상식 audience 청중

M Hey, Marcy. What's the matter?

W I'm working on an essay for my history course, and I can't find the research I need at the library.

M Maybe you should ask a librarian to help.

W I tried that. They can't do anything for me.

M I don't know what else to tell you.

W It's hopeless. I'm going to get an F, I just know it.

M Hey, don't worry. There must be something you can do.

W Maybe. I'm just fed up with the whole thing.

남 이봐, Marcy. 무슨 일이야?

여 역사 수업에 낼 에세이를 쓰고 있는데, 내가 필요한 자료를 도서관에서 찾을 수가 없어.

남 사서에게 도움을 요청해 볼 수 있을 거야.

여 해봤어. 날 위해서 아무것도 해줄 수 없대.

남 달리 무슨 말을 해야 할지 모르겠다.

여 가망이 없어. 난 F를 받을 거야. 난 그냥 알아.

남 야, 걱정하지 마. 네가 할 수 있는 일이 뭔가 있을 거야.

여 그럴지도 모르지. 난 그냥 이 모든 것에 질려 버렸어.

Vocabulary	research 연구 자료 librarian 사서 hopeless 가망 없는 be fed up with ~에 질리다 whole 전체의
	content 만족한 frustrated 좌절한

M Hey, Jen. Are you coming to quiz night?

W I've decided I should study tonight instead.

M Really? It's going to be great. You can win free stuff, like food and drinks and prizes.

W Sounds great. It's at the Old Town Restaurant, right?

M Yes, from 7:30−9:30 every Wednesday night.

W Every week, huh? Well, how about I come next week?

남 안녕, Jen. 퀴즈의 밤에 올 거니?

여 오늘 밤엔 대신 공부를 해야 한다고 결심했어.

남 정말? 아주 재미있을 텐데. 음식, 음료수, 상품 같은 공짜 물건을 딸 수 있어.

여 그거 정말 좋다. Old Town 식당에서 하는 거 맞지?

남 그래, 7시 반부터 9시 반까지 매주 수요일 밤에 열려.

여 매주라고? 음, 그러면 내가 다음 주에 가면 어떨까?

M That'd be great. Oh, and students <u>get in</u> <u>free</u>, by the way.

남 그거 좋지. 오, 그건 그렇고 학생들은 무료로 입장할 수 있대.

Vocabulary | trivia 일반 상식   stuff 물건   prize 상품

W My parents began to homeschool me at a <u>young age</u>. They don't like a lot of what teachers teach in <u>public</u> schools. Also, they don't want me to be around kids who might <u>get me into trouble</u>. Home school isn't so bad. I don't get to see my friends every day, but I <u>still see</u> them on the weekends. My parents say that when I am a teenager, I can <u>choose to</u> go back to a public school if I want. But I <u>haven't decided</u> whether I want to or not.

여 우리 부모님은 나를 어린 나이에 홈스쿨링을 받게 하기 시작하셨다. 그분들은 공립 학교에서 교사들이 가르치는 많은 것들을 좋아하지 않는다. 또한 그들은 날 곤경에 빠뜨릴 수 있는 아이들 주위에 내가 있기를 원하지 않는다. 홈스쿨링은 그다지 나쁘지 않다. 나는 매일 친구들을 만나지는 못하지만 주말에 아직도 그들을 만난다. 부모님은 내가 십대가 되면 내가 원할 경우 공립 학교로 돌아가는 것을 선택할 수 있다고 말씀하신다. 하지만 나는 아직 내가 그러고 싶은지 아닌지 결정하지 못했다.

Vocabulary | homeschool 홈스쿨링을 하다   public 공립의   teenager 십대   choose to ~하기를 선택하다
go back to ~로 돌아가다   whether ~ or not ~인지 아닌지

UNIT XI HAVE YOU EVER BEEN ON A DIET?

Check Up

p.67

01 a   **02** 1.F 2.T 3.T

03 **A** <u>How many times</u> have you been to the theater?

B Actually, <u>I've never been</u> before.

A Oh, is this <u>your first time</u>? You must be excited.

B Yes, I've always wanted to go.

Check Up Scripts

01

a. **M** I'd like to check out now, please.

W Of course. Your total is $12.

b. **M** Can you direct me to the store?

W Sure. It's right down the street.

c. **M** Would you like to go to the store?

W Sure. I need to do some shopping.

a. **남** 계산하고 싶은데요.

여 네. 총액은 12달러입니다.

b. **남** 가게로 가는 길 좀 알려줄래?

여 그럼. 그건 바로 길 저 아래에 있어.

c. **남** 가게에 갈래?

여 좋지. 쇼핑을 좀 해야 해.

Vocabulary | check out 계산하다   total 총액   direct 방향을 알려주다

W Have you ever been to a fashion show?
M No, I haven't. What is it?
W It's when models show off new kinds of clothing.
M Sounds like fun. I'd like to go sometime.
W There's a show this weekend. Want to come with me?
M Sure. I'll see you then.

여 패션쇼에 가본 적 있어?
남 아니, 안 가봤어. 그게 뭔데?
여 모델들이 새로운 종류의 옷을 보여주는 때야.
남 재미있겠다. 언제 가보고 싶어.
여 이번 주말에 쇼가 있어. 같이 갈래?
남 좋지. 그때 보자.

Vocabulary	clothing 옷, 의류

03

A How many times have you been to the theater?
B Actually, I've never been before.
A Oh, is this your first time? You must be excited.
B Yes, I've always wanted to go.

A 그 극장에 얼마나 여러 번 가봤어?
B 사실 한 번도 가본 적이 없어.
A 오, 그럼 이번이 처음이야? 신나겠다.
B 응, 언제나 가보고 싶었어.

Vocabulary	theater 극장

Actual Test

1 ③   2 ③   3 ②   4 ⑤   5 ⑤   6 ③   7 ④   8 ① | p.68

W Dear Diary: Today was a really fun day. First, I took a long walk with my dog, Spot. We went to the park and played. Then we sat down on the grass for a picnic lunch. I saw some of my friends there, too, so we played a game of Frisbee afterward.

여 오늘의 일기: 오늘은 정말 즐거운 날이었다. 우선 나는 내 개 Spot과 함께 오랫동안 산책을 했다. 우리는 공원에 가서 놀았다. 그러고 나서 우리는 잔디밭에 앉아서 소풍 도시락을 먹었다. 나는 거기서 내 친구들도 몇 명 보았고, 그래서 우리는 그 후에 원반 던지기 게임을 했다.

Vocabulary	picnic lunch 소풍 도시락	Frisbee 원반 던지기	afterward 그 후에

M Are you ready to go out for dinner, Rosa?
W Not quite yet.
M OK, I can wait. Have you ever been to this restaurant?
W No, it's my first time. What's it like?
M Oh, you're going to love it. They have the

남 저녁 먹으러 나갈 준비 됐어, Rosa?
여 아직 안 됐어.
남 알겠어, 기다릴게. 이 식당에 가본 적 있어?
여 아니, 처음이야. 어떤데?
남 오, 너 정말 좋아할 거야. 생선 요리가 최고야.

best fish.

W Cool. What about <u>vegetarian</u> <u>dishes</u>?

M I think they have them, but I'm not sure.

W You might want <u>to call</u> them and <u>ask</u>.

M Sure, I'll do that while you're getting ready.

여 멋지다. 채식 요리는 어때?

남 있을 것 같은데 확실치는 않아.

여 한번 전화해서 물어보지 그래.

남 좋아, 네가 준비하는 동안 그렇게 할게.

Vocabulary	vegetarian 채식주의자; 채식의 dish 요리

3

W Have you ever wanted to <u>look</u> different? Lots of young people are not happy with <u>the</u> <u>way</u> <u>they</u> <u>look</u>. Sometimes, this can become very <u>unhealthy</u>. For example, some people <u>stop</u> <u>eating</u> to be thin. But this can cause serious <u>health</u> <u>problems</u>, and even death. It's much better to just <u>be</u> <u>satisfied</u> <u>with</u> the way you look. You are special and unique. Why try to <u>change</u> <u>who</u> <u>you</u> <u>are</u>?

여 달라 보이고 싶은 적이 있었나요? 많은 젊은이들이 그들의 외모에 만족하지 않습니다. 때로 이것은 건강에 매우 나쁘게 될 수 있습니다. 예를 들어, 어떤 사람들은 날씬해지기 위해 먹는 것을 그만둡니다. 하지만 이것은 심각한 건강 문제를 일으킬 수 있고 심지어 죽음에 이를 수도 있습니다. 자신의 외모에 대해 그냥 만족하는 것이 훨씬 낫습니다. 당신은 특별하고 독특합니다. 왜 자신을 바꾸려고 하나요?

Vocabulary	unhealthy 건강에 나쁜 thin 날씬한 serious 심각한 be satisfied with ~에 만족하다 unique 독특한

4

W Sam, we need to talk about <u>your</u> <u>grades</u>.

M I know. They aren't very good right now.

W According to your report card, you got a C <u>in</u> <u>science</u>.

M I <u>did</u> <u>poorly</u> on the exams. But I'll study more. But I did get an A <u>in</u> <u>math</u>.

W That's good. But you still need to <u>try</u> <u>harder</u> in other classes, like history. You got a C⁻!

M You're right; I'll do better. But <u>just</u> <u>look</u> <u>at</u> my English grade.

W An A⁻ is very good. As is an A in Art class. I guess I can't be <u>too</u> <u>disappointed</u>.

M I promise my grades <u>will</u> <u>improve</u>.

여 Sam. 우리 네 성적에 대해 이야기를 해야겠다.

남 알아요. 지금은 성적이 별로 좋지 않죠.

여 성적표에 따르면 너는 과학에서 C를 받았어.

남 시험을 망쳤어요. 하지만 더 많이 공부할게요. 하지만 수학에서는 A를 받았어요.

여 그건 좋아. 하지만 역사 같은 다른 수업에서는 여전히 더 노력해야겠다. 넌 C⁻를 받았어!

남 맞아요. 더 잘 할게요. 하지만 제 영어 성적을 보세요.

여 A⁻는 아주 좋아. 미술 수업에서 A를 받은 것도 그렇고. 너무 실망할 수는 없겠구나.

남 성적이 올라갈 거라고 약속할게요.

Vocabulary	grade 성적 report card 성적표 poorly 형편없이 disappointed 실망한 promise 약속하다 improve 향상되다

5

W Are you <u>trying</u> <u>out</u> <u>for</u> the football team this year?

M Yes. In fact, tryouts are next week.

여 너 올해 미식축구 팀에 지원할 거야?

남 응. 사실 테스트가 다음 주야.

W Good luck then. What position do you want to play?

여 그럼 행운을 빌게. 어느 위치에서 뛰고 싶어?

M I want to be a linebacker, but I don't think I can.

남 수비수가 되고 싶은데 할 수 있을 것 같지 않아.

W And why is that?

여 왜 그런데?

M I need to gain some weight, I think.

남 체중을 좀 늘려야 할 것 같아.

W Yes, if you want to play defense, you have to be big.

여 그래. 수비수가 되고 싶으면 덩치가 커야지.

M Yeah. I think I'm just too skinny for it.

남 맞아. 나는 그러기엔 너무 마른 것 같아.

W Have you tried eating a lot?

여 많이 먹는 것 시도해 봤어?

M I think that's what I'll have to do.

남 그게 내가 해야 하는 일인 것 같아.

Vocabulary	try out for (선발을 위해) 지원하다 tryout (선발을 위한) 테스트 position 위치 gain weight 체중을 늘리다
	defense 수비 skinny 마른

M It was Jake's first day of high school. Jake had never been to a real high school before. He had only been to home school his whole life. So when his parents decided to put him in a public school, he was very nervous. To make things easier, he decided to make a new friend. He found someone who looked friendly and approached him. In this situation, what will Jake say?

남 Jake의 고등학교 등교 첫 날이었다. Jake는 진짜 고등학교에 와본 적이 없었다. 그는 평생 동안 홈스쿨링만 했다. 그래서 그의 부모님이 그를 공립 학교에 보내기로 결정했을 때 그는 매우 긴장되었다. 상황을 쉽게 만들기 위해 그는 새 친구를 사귀기로 했다. 그는 상냥해 보이는 어떤 아이를 발견하고 그에게로 다가갔다. 이런 상황에서 Jake는 뭐라고 말하겠는가?

Vocabulary	public school 공립 학교 nervous 긴장된, 초조한 approach 다가가다

W Hey, Chris. What's your favorite movie?

여 이봐. Chris. 네가 제일 좋아하는 영화는 뭐야?

M I love all the "Harry Potter" movies the best.

남 나는 'Harry Potter' 시리즈의 모든 영화들을 제일 좋아해.

W Really? How many times have you seen them?

여 정말? 몇 번이나 봤는데?

M More times than I can count.

남 셀 수 있는 것보다 많이.

W Well, I envy you. I like them too, but I've yet to see them all.

여 음. 네가 부럽다. 나도 그것들을 좋아하는데 아직 다 보지 못했어.

M Oh, you simply must! They are so much fun.

남 오. 너 꼭 봐야 해! 정말 재미있어.

W Maybe we can watch them together sometime.

여 언젠가 같이 볼 수도 있겠다.

M That sounds like a lot of fun.

남 정말 재미있겠는걸.

8

W Have you ever been on a diet, Mike?	여 다이어트 해본 적 있어, Mike?
M I was on a diet a few years ago. Why?	남 몇 년 전에 다이어트 했었어. 왜?
W I just started one. This is my first time trying it.	여 막 시작했거든. 이번이 처음 해보는 거야.
M Oh. Why would you need to be on a diet?	남 오. 네가 왜 다이어트를 해야 하지?
W I just want to lose a little bit of weight.	여 그냥 체중을 좀 줄이고 싶어.
M But you look great already!	남 하지만 넌 이미 멋진데!
W You're very sweet, but I want to be good-looking, like the models on TV.	여 그렇게 말해줘서 고마워. 하지만 난 멋져 보이고 싶어. TV에 나오는 모델들처럼 말이야.
M If you ask me, they're too skinny. You're great just the way you are.	남 내 생각을 묻는다면 그들은 너무 말랐어. 넌 딱 지금 이대로가 좋아.

UNIT XII WHAT WOULD YOU DO IF YOU WERE PRESIDENT?

✺ Check Up

p.73

01 b

02

	Rural	Urban
Where many, many people live		✓
Where farms are located	✓	
Where a lot of business takes place		✓

03 A Hey, John. What would you do if you were president?

   B If I were president, I would make every day a holiday!

   A Wow, I wish you really were the president!

Check Up Scripts

01

M What would you do to improve the community?	남 너는 지역사회를 더 좋게 만들기 위해 뭘 하겠어?
W I would do more to help poor people.	여 가난한 사람들을 돕기 위해 더 많은 일을 할 거야.

M I agree. I would start a soup kitchen to feed them.	**남** 동감이야. 나는 그들에게 음식을 주기 위해 무료 급식소를 시작할 거야.
W Great idea. I think I would start a charity group.	**여** 좋은 생각이야. 나는 자선단체를 시작할까 해.
M What would the charity do?	**남** 그 자선단체는 뭘 할 건데?
W Give used clothes to the poor, I think.	**여** 가난한 사람들에게 헌 옷을 나누어 주는 게 어떨까 해.

02

M There are two kinds of communities. Urban communities are mainly cities. They have high populations and lots of businesses. Rural communities are in the country. There you'll find things like farms and ranches. What type of community would you live in?	**남** 두 종류의 지역사회가 있습니다. 도시 지역사회는 대부분 도시입니다. 거기에는 높은 인구와 많은 사업이 있습니다. 전원 지역사회는 시골에 있습니다. 거기서는 농장이나 목장 같은 것들을 볼 수 있습니다. 여러분은 어떤 종류의 지역사회에 살고 싶습니까?

03

A Hey, John. What would you do if you were president?	**A** 야. John. 네가 대통령이라면 넌 뭘 할 거야?
B If I were president, I would make every day a holiday!	**B** 내가 대통령이라면 난 모든 날을 휴일로 만들겠어!
A Wow, I wish you really were the president!	**A** 와, 네가 정말 대통령이면 좋겠다!

Actual Test   1 ②   2 ④   3 ③   4 ②   5 ⑤   6 ②   7 ③   8 ② | p.74

W I think I want to be a public official one day.	**여** 나는 언젠가 공무원이 되고 싶은 것 같아.
M It's a lot of hard work, but I'm sure you can do it.	**남** 그건 아주 어려운 일이지만 넌 분명 잘 할 수 있을 거야.
W Thanks. I've always been a natural leader.	**여** 고마워. 나는 언제나 타고난 지도자였거든.
M What would you do if you became an official?	**남** 네가 공무원이 되면 뭘 할 건데?
W I would fight for people's rights, I think.	**여** 사람들의 권리를 위해 싸울 것 같아.
M That's a very noble cause. Good luck with your dream!	**남** 그건 정말 고귀한 명분이다. 네 꿈을 이루길 빌게!

Vocabulary	public official 공무원 natural 타고난 leader 지도자 fight for ~을 위해 싸우다 rights 권리
	noble 고귀한, 숭고한 cause 대의 명분

2

M Hey, Lisa. You should come to the charity drive this Sunday.

W OK. What's the charity for?

M It's to benefit the poor. You can donate food, clothes, or toys.

W Hm. I don't know what to bring.

M Well, what would you want if you were poor?

W I'll think about that. What time is the event?

M It's from 9:00–11:00 at the community center.

W OK. I'll see you there. Want to get some lunch afterward?

M No need. There will be free hotdogs for everyone.

남 안녕, Lisa. 이번 일요일에 자선 물품 행사에 와야 해.

여 알겠어. 뭘 위한 자선 행사야?

남 가난한 사람들을 돕기 위한 거야. 음식, 옷, 아니면 장난감을 기부할 수 있어.

여 흠. 뭘 가져가야 할지 모르겠네.

남 음. 네가 가난하다면 뭘 원할 것 같아?

여 생각해 봐야겠다. 행사가 몇 시야?

남 지역 회관에서 9시부터 11까지야.

여 좋아. 거기서 보자. 끝나고 나서 점심 먹을래?

남 그럴 필요 없어. 모두를 위한 무료 핫도그가 있을 거야.

Vocabulary	charity drive 자선 물품 행사 benefit ~을 이롭게 하다 donate 기부하다

3

W I can't wait to visit our family this weekend!

M Me too. I wish we could do it more often.

W Do you have our tickets?

M Yes, I have them here. They are window seats, like we asked.

W Great. And what time do we leave?

M The departure time is 12:30.

W So we should be there two hours early.

M That's a good idea. We'll have to search for our gate.

W I hope I don't get air sick, like last time!

여 이번 주말에 우리 가족을 방문하는 게 너무 기다려져!

남 나도야. 좀 더 자주 할 수 있었으면 좋겠어.

여 우리 표 가지고 있어?

남 응. 여기 있어. 우리가 요청했듯이 창가 좌석이야.

여 좋아. 몇 시에 출발해?

남 출발 시각은 12시 30분이야.

여 그러면 두 시간 전에 가 있어야겠다.

남 좋은 생각이야. 탑승구를 찾아야 할 거니까.

여 내가 지난번처럼 비행기 멀미를 하지 말아야 할 텐데!

Vocabulary	departure 출발 search for ~을 찾다 gate 탑승구 air sick 비행기 멀미를 하는

4

M Most farms are found far away from cities. This means that fruit and vegetables are more expensive and less fresh in the city. Well, a few years ago I decided to do something

남 대부분의 농장은 도시로부터 멀리 떨어져 있습니다. 이것은 과일과 야채가 도시에서는 더 비싸고 덜 신선하다는 것을 의미합니다. 음, 몇 년 전에 저는 이것을 돕기 위한 무언가를 하기로 마음먹었습니다. 저는 제 아파트 건물 옥상에

to help this. I planted a garden <u>on the roof</u> of my apartment building. Since then, I've helped others <u>do the same</u>. Now, there is <u>a big market</u> for fresh, local vegetables. Still, <u>I wish</u> more people would <u>join our movement</u>.

정원을 만들었습니다. 그때부터 저는 다른 사람들도 같은 일을 하도록 돕고 있습니다. 이제 신선한 지역 채소를 위한 커다란 시장이 열립니다. 그래도 전 더 많은 사람들이 우리의 운동에 동참하기를 바랍니다.

> **Vocabulary** local 지역의   join 동참하다   movement (사회적) 운동

5

W Hey, Simon. Are you going to the concert tonight?

여 야, Simon. 너 오늘 밤 공연에 갈 거니?

M <u>I would go</u> if I didn't have so much homework.

남 숙제가 그렇게 많지 않다면 갈 텐데 말이야.

W You should really try. It's <u>for charity</u>, after all.

여 꼭 가봐야 해. 어쨌든 자선을 위한 거잖아.

M I'll <u>do my best</u>. What time does it start?

남 최선을 다할게. 몇 시에 시작하지?

W It begins at 7:00.

여 7시에 시작해.

M OK. How about meeting <u>an hour early</u>?

남 알겠어. 한 시간 전에 만나는 게 어때?

W That's not so good. I'm helping <u>to sell tickets</u>.

여 그건 별로야. 난 입장권 판매를 도울 거라서.

M OK. I'll find you a <u>half-hour into</u> the concert then.

남 알았어. 그럼 공연 시작하고 나서 30분 후에 만나자.

W Great! I hope to see you there.

여 좋아! 거기서 보길 바라.

> **Vocabulary** after all 어쨌든, 결국

6

M Today, two young boys were given an award <u>for their service</u> to the community. For months, the boys have been <u>picking up garbage</u> from the roads and sidewalks in our town. They say that <u>awards are nice</u>, but the real reward is helping <u>keep their town clean</u>.

남 오늘 두 어린 소년이 지역사회를 위한 공헌으로 상을 받았습니다. 몇 달 동안 그 소년들은 우리 도시의 도로와 인도에서 쓰레기를 주워 왔습니다. 그들은 상이 멋지지만 진짜 보상은 그들의 도시를 깨끗하게 하는 것을 돕는 것이라고 말합니다.

> **Vocabulary** award 상   service 공헌, 활동   garbage 쓰레기   sidewalk 인도   reward 보상

7

M I hear you've been doing <u>charity work</u>, Jan.

남 네가 자선 활동을 해왔다고 들었어. Jan.

W Yes. Some friends and I started a program for <u>old people</u>.

여 그래. 친구들 몇 명과 나는 노인들을 위한 프로그램을 시작했어.

M That's very kind of you. What do you do?

남 그거 정말 친절한 일이다. 뭘 하는데?

W We <u>organize activities</u> for them at the community center.

여 우리는 지역 회관에서 그분들을 위한 활동을 조직해.

M Neat. It's really important to take care <u>of</u> <u>our</u> elders.

W I agree. And we've gotten <u>a</u> <u>lot</u> <u>of</u> <u>support</u> from the community.

M Really?

W Yes. We <u>couldn't</u> <u>have</u> <u>done</u> it without their help.

M Well, best of <u>luck</u> <u>going</u> <u>forward</u>.

Vocabulary	senior citizen 노인 organize 조직하다 activity 활동 take care of ~을 돌보다 elder 연장자 support 대의 지원

남 멋지네. 어르신들을 돌보는 것은 정말 중요한 일이지.

여 나도 그렇게 생각해. 그리고 우리는 지역사회로부터 많은 지원을 받았어.

남 정말?

여 응. 그들의 도움이 없었다면 우린 그 일을 하지 못했을 거야.

남 음, 앞으로도 행운을 빌게.

① **M** Would you like to join me for a nice dinner downtown?

   W <u>I</u> <u>would</u> <u>if</u> I didn't have to work late tonight.

② **M** What would you do <u>if</u> <u>you</u> <u>were</u> rich?

   W No, I don't make much money at my job.

③ **M** I hear there is a <u>charity</u> <u>event</u> at the park today.

   W We should go! <u>I</u> <u>love</u> <u>helping</u> the community.

④ **M** Did you enjoy the book that I lent you?

   W It was so good that I read <u>the</u> <u>whole</u> <u>thing</u> in a day.

⑤ **M** What's the matter with Cathy? <u>She</u> <u>seems</u> <u>sad</u>.

   W I know. She <u>acts</u> <u>as</u> <u>if</u> everyone dislikes her.

Vocabulary	act 행동하다 dislike 싫어하다

① **남** 시내에서 멋진 저녁 식사 같이 할래?

   여 오늘 밤에 야근해야 하지 않으면 그럴 텐데.

② **남** 네가 부자라면 뭘 하겠어?

   여 아니, 내 일은 보수가 많지 않아.

③ **남** 오늘 공원에서 자선 행사가 있다고 들었어.

   여 가봐야겠다! 나는 지역사회를 돕는 게 정말 좋아.

④ **남** 내가 빌려준 책 재미있었어?

   여 너무 좋아서 하루에 다 읽었어.

⑤ **남** Cathy 왜 그래? 속상해 보여.

   여 알아. 그 애는 마치 모든 사람이 자기를 싫어하는 것처럼 행동해.

모의고사 1회

| 01 ④ | 02 ② | 03 ⑤ | 04 ③ | 05 ① | 06 ② | 07 ⑤ | 08 ③ | 09 ④ | 10 ① |
| 11 ③ | 12 ① | 13 ③ | 14 ③ | 15 ⑤ | 16 ① | 17 ④ | 18 ① | 19 ③ | 20 ② |

01

M When ships are at sea, they sometimes communicate with one another using flags. There are 26 flags in all, and all of them have a different meaning. For instance, a flag with a small square in the center, surrounded by two larger squares, means that the ship needs medical assistance.

남 배들이 바다에 있을 때 그들은 가끔 깃발을 사용해서 의사소통을 합니다. 전부 합쳐 26개의 깃발이 있는데 그들 모두가 각기 다른 의미를 갖고 있습니다. 예를 들어 두 개의 더 큰 정사각형으로 둘러싸인 작은 정사각형이 있는 깃발은 그 배가 의료 지원을 필요로 한다는 것을 의미합니다.

02

W Hi, Mark. My name is Susan.

M Yes, I remember you. You're new to this school, right?

W Yes, I just started yesterday. Are you going to science class?

M Yes, I'm on my way there now.

W Do you mind if I walk with you?

M Of course not. Come along.

W Thanks. I'm afraid I don't know my way around yet.

M Well, I'm happy to show you the way. I could even give you a tour later, if you like.

여 안녕, Mark. 내 이름은 Susan이야.

남 응. 나 너 기억해. 이 학교에 새로 왔지?

여 그래, 바로 어제 시작했어. 과학 수업에 가는 거니?

남 응. 지금 거기 가는 길이야.

여 내가 너랑 같이 걸어가도 될까?

남 당연히 되지. 같이 가자.

여 고마워. 아직 길을 잘 몰라서.

남 어, 네게 기꺼이 길을 보여줄게. 네가 좋다면 나중에 같이 한 바퀴 둘러볼 수도 있어.

03

M Beth, do you have a moment to talk?

W Of course, Mr. Ling. What's the matter?

M I wanted to talk to you about your grade in my class.

W I'm not doing very well, am I?

M Well, you failed the last test, and I'm a little concerned.

W Do you have any tips on how I might do better?

남 Beth. 잠깐 이야기할 시간 있니?

여 그럼요, Ling 선생님. 무슨 일인데요?

남 내 수업에서 네 성적에 대해 이야기하고 싶었어.

여 제가 잘 못 하고 있죠, 그런가요?

남 음. 너는 지난 시험에서 낙제했어. 그래서 난 좀 걱정이 된단다.

여 어떻게 하면 제가 더 잘 할 수 있는지에 대해서 조언해 주실 것이 있으세요?

M	There is a study group after school. I think it would really help. You should join.	남	방과 후에 하는 스터디 모임이 있어. 내 생각에 그게 정말 도움이 될 거 같아. 네가 함께 했으면 해.
W	I'd be delighted to join.	여	함께 하면 정말 좋을 것 같아요.
M	OK. We meet at 4:00. Will I see you there?	남	좋아. 우리는 4시에 만난단다. 거기서 널 볼 수 있지?

04

W	Yet another robbery was reported last night on the south side of the city. This time, a clothing store was broken into, and many items were stolen. This is the fourth time this week that a robbery occurred in this part of town. Though they have no clues, authorities are confident that the criminals will be found.	여	어젯밤에 도시 남쪽에서 또 다른 강도 사건이 보고되었습니다. 이번에는 옷 가게가 침입을 당해서 많은 물건들이 도난당했습니다. 이것은 이번 주 들어 도시의 이 지역에서 강도 사건이 네 번째로 발생한 것입니다. 실마리를 잡지 못하고 있지만 당국은 범인들을 곧 찾게 될 것이라고 확신하고 있습니다.

05

W	Hi, Jim. Are you enjoying your holiday?	여	안녕. Jim. 휴일을 즐기고 있니?
M	Sure, it's nice to have time to relax.	남	그럼. 쉴 시간이 있어서 좋아.
W	What are you doing to pass the time?	여	뭘 하면서 시간을 보내고 있어?
M	Actually, I'm not doing much. To tell the truth, I'm kind of bored.	남	사실 별로 하는 게 없어. 사실을 말하자면 조금 지루해.
W	Well, I have a hobby that keeps me busy. Maybe you should get one, too.	여	음, 나는 나를 바쁘게 하는 취미가 있어. 너도 취미를 하나 가져야 할 것 같아.
M	That's a good idea. But which should I choose?	남	그거 좋은 생각이야. 하지만 내가 뭘 선택해야 할까?
W	I enjoy photography. I can teach you sometime.	여	나는 사진을 좋아해. 내가 언제 너한테 가르쳐줄 수 있어.
M	That's great. Thanks!	남	그거 좋네. 고마워!

06

M	Hey, Lisa. We should meet soon to talk about our class project.	남	안녕. Lisa. 우리 수업 프로젝트에 대해 이야기하기 위해서 곧 만나야겠어.
W	I agree. I'm free Tuesday if you are.	여	좋아. 네가 된다면 난 화요일에 한가해.
M	I would, but I have baseball practice that afternoon.	남	그러면 좋겠는데 그날 오후에 야구 연습이 있어.
W	OK. How about Friday, then?	여	좋아. 그럼 금요일은 어때?
M	I don't know. The project is due on Monday.	남	모르겠네. 프로젝트가 월요일까지잖아.
W	How long will it take to complete it?	여	그걸 완성하는 데 얼마나 걸릴까?
M	We should begin about five days before it is due.	남	마감일로부터 5일 전쯤 시작해야 해.
W	OK, if that's what it takes, we'll meet then.	여	좋아. 그만큼 시간이 걸린다면 그때 만나자.

07

W These days, kids spend a lot of time at home. They play video games, watch movies, surf the internet. It's easy to see why it's so much fun to stay in. But it can also be quite unhealthy. Kids who stay indoors all the time are more likely to gain weight. This can be quite dangerous to you. So go play sports, go hiking, take a walk—anything to get outdoors and stay healthy.

여 오늘날 아이들은 많은 시간을 집에서 보냅니다. 그들은 비디오 게임을 하고, 영화를 보고, 인터넷 서핑을 합니다. 집에 있는 것이 왜 그렇게 재미있는지 알기는 쉽습니다. 하지만 그것은 또한 건강에 무척 안 좋을 수 있습니다. 항상 실내에 있는 아이들은 체중이 늘기가 쉽습니다. 이것은 여러분에게 매우 위험할 수 있습니다. 그러니 운동 경기를 하든, 하이킹을 하든, 산책을 하든 무엇이든 밖에 있을 수 있는 것을 하고 건강을 유지하세요.

08

M I've always loved animals. When I was a kid, I rescued abandoned pets all the time and tried to help them. As I got older, I took an interest in medical science. One day I realized that I could make a career out of putting those two passions together. Today, I have the job I've always wanted. I get to help animals, and I get to work in medicine.

남 저는 언제나 동물을 좋아했어요. 어렸을 때 저는 항상 버려진 애완동물들을 구해주고 그들을 도우려고 노력했죠. 나이가 들면서 저는 의학에 관심을 갖게 됐어요. 어느 날 저는 제가 이 두 가지 열정을 결합해서 진로를 개척할 수 있다는 것을 깨달았습니다. 오늘날 저는 제가 언제나 원했던 일을 하고 있어요. 저는 동물들을 도울 수 있고 의학 분야에서 일하게 됐습니다.

09

W What would you like to do during our camping trip?

M We're going to be in the mountains, so we should definitely do some rock climbing.

W I agree. I also want to go hiking in the woods.

M That sounds great. I think we should take up mountain biking, as well.

W Yes! I've always wanted to do that.

M I can't wait to leave!

여 우리 캠핑 여행 때 뭘 하고 싶어?

남 우린 산에 갈 거잖아. 그러니까 암벽 등반을 꼭 해야 해.

여 나도 그렇게 생각해. 나는 또 숲 속에서 하이킹도 하고 싶어.

남 그거 좋겠다. 내 생각엔 산악 자전거도 해보면 좋을 것 같은데.

여 그래! 나 항상 그거 해보고 싶었어.

남 빨리 떠나고 싶다!

10

M Did you hear about the big sale this weekend?

W No. What kind of sale is it?

M The electronics store is reducing its prices by 25%, for one day only.

W Wow, that's awfully generous. Do you mind if I join you?

M Sure. Meet me there in the morning around 8:00.

남 이번 주말에 하는 큰 세일에 대해서 들었어?

여 아니. 어떤 종류의 세일인데?

남 전자제품 가게에서 딱 하루 동안만 가격을 25% 인하한대.

여 와, 그거 진짜 후하다. 내가 같이 가도 돼?

남 그럼. 아침 8시쯤에 거기서 만나자.

W	OK. I'll be there.	여	그래. 거기서 봐.
M	You'd better not be late. All the best items won't be there for long.	남	늦지 않는 게 좋을 거야. 제일 좋은 물건들은 오래 남아 있지 않을 거야.
W	We'll try to be the first people there then.	여	그럼 제일 먼저 가는 사람들이 되도록 해보자.

11

W	Are you interested in joining the science club, Kyle?	여	과학 동아리에 드는 것에 관심 있어, Kyle?
M	Yes, I'd love to be a member of the club.	남	응. 난 그 동아리 회원이 되고 싶어.
W	Well, I'm already a member, so I got a memo today about the next meeting.	여	음. 난 이미 회원이라서 오늘 모임에 대한 쪽지를 받았어.
M	When is it? I'd like to attend.	남	언제야? 나도 참석하고 싶어.
W	It's on Tuesday, at 1:00 in the afternoon. Can you make it?	여	화요일 오후 1시야. 너 올 수 있어?
M	I'll be there. Where is the meeting being held?	남	갈게. 모임이 어디에서 열려?
W	In the science lab, of course!	여	당연히 과학 실험실이지!

12

M	Hey, Cathy. What's the matter?	남	이봐. Cathy. 무슨 일 있어?
W	I'm supposed to write a report for history class.	여	역사 수업에 낼 보고서를 써야 해.
M	Are you having trouble with it?	남	무슨 문제라도 있니?
W	Yeah. I'm just not that interested in the subject.	여	응. 난 그냥 그 과목에 그다지 관심이 없어.
M	I think history is exciting. I love learning about the past.	남	난 역사가 흥미롭다고 생각해. 과거에 대해서 배우는 게 정말 좋아.
W	Well, that makes one of us. I almost fall asleep every time I open a history book.	여	흠. 난 안 그래. 난 역사책을 펼 때마다 거의 잠이 들 뻔해.
M	Maybe you just need a topic that interests you.	남	어쩌면 넌 네 관심을 끌 주제가 필요한 건지도 몰라.
W	I've tried all kinds of topics. I just can't seem to get very excited about it.	여	온갖 종류의 주제를 시도해 봤어. 난 그냥 그것에 대해서 흥미를 갖지 못하는 것 같아.

13

W	Excuse me. I've been waiting here forever. Is there some problem?	여	실례합니다. 저 여기서 한참 기다렸는데요. 무슨 문제가 있나요?
M	I'm afraid so. There is some damage to the tracks.	남	그런 것 같습니다. 트랙에 손상이 있어서요.
W	What does that mean for all of us passengers?	여	그건 우리 승객 전체에게 어떤 의미가 되는 건가요?

| M | Right now, there is a 1-hour delay. | 남 | 지금으로서는 한 시간 지연됩니다. |
| M | | | |

14

| M | Do you remember our first date, Marie? | 남 | 우리 첫 데이트 기억해, Marie? |

M	Right now, there is a 1-hour delay.	남	지금으로서는 한 시간 지연됩니다.
W	Are you serious? I have to be across town in 30 minutes.	여	정말로요? 전 30분 안에 도시를 가로질러 가야 한다고요.
M	You could take a bus, I suppose.	남	버스를 타실 수도 있겠죠.
W	Never mind. I already paid my fare. I'll just wait here in the station.	여	신경 쓰지 마세요. 전 벌써 요금을 냈어요. 여기 역에서 그냥 기다릴게요.
M	OK. It's your choice. I'll let you know as soon as the problem is fixed.	남	그러세요. 고객님의 선택이니까요. 문제가 해결되는 대로 바로 알려드리겠습니다.

14

M	Do you remember our first date, Marie?	남	우리 첫 데이트 기억해, Marie?
W	Of course I remember. It's one of my happiest memories.	여	당연히 기억하지. 제일 행복했던 기억 중 하나인데.
M	We went to a little Italian restaurant downtown.	남	우리는 시내에 있는 작은 이탈리아 식당에 갔었지.
W	Yes, it was very romantic. But the food was awful.	여	그래. 아주 낭만적이었어. 하지만 음식은 형편없었지.
M	I'd forgotten about that. I was a little embarrassed.	남	그것에 대해선 잊어버렸었네. 난 약간 당황했었어.
W	And then afterward, we took a walk in the park.	여	그리고 그 다음에는 공원에 가서 산책을 했지.
M	It was a cool autumn evening, if I remember correctly.	남	서늘한 가을날 저녁이었어. 내 기억이 맞으면 말이야.
W	That's right. You offered me your coat because I was cold.	여	맞아. 내가 추워서 네가 네 코트를 나에게 줬잖아.

15

W	I baked some cookies for the party this evening.	여	오늘 저녁 파티를 위해 과자를 좀 구웠어.
M	Great. I'll put them with all the other snacks.	남	잘 했네. 다른 간식들과 같이 놓을게.
W	I don't think it turned out to be very good, though.	여	그런데 별로 잘 된 것 같지는 않아.
M	Why do you say that? They look fine.	남	왜 그렇게 말해? 맛있어 보이는데.
W	Well, I forgot about them, and left them in the oven for too long.	여	음. 그것들에 대해서 잊어버려서 오븐에 너무 오랫동안 놔뒀어.
M	They don't seem to be burned at all.	남	전혀 탄 것처럼 보이지는 않는걸.
W	Still, I don't think they're my best cookies.	여	그래도 내가 제일 잘 만든 과자는 아닌 것 같아.

16

M   Joseph hurried to get ready for school. He had overslept, and now he was about to miss his bus to school. Like most mornings, Joseph's mother wants him to sit down and eat breakfast. But he knows that if he does, he will miss his bus. In this situation, what is Joseph likely to say to his mother?

남   Joseph는 서둘러 등교 준비를 했다. 그는 늦잠을 자서 이제 학교로 가는 버스를 놓치기 직전이었다. 대부분의 아침처럼 Joseph의 어머니는 그가 앉아서 아침을 먹길 원한다. 그러나 그는 만약 그런다면 버스를 놓칠 거라는 걸 알고 있다. 이런 상황에서 Joseph는 어머니에게 뭐라고 말하겠는가?

17

W   Excuse me. Where can I find the bank? I need to open a checking account.

M   Go to the end of Market Street and turn left.

W   OK. What do I do then?

M   Turn right at the second road, near the school.

W   And where do I go after that?

M   Go straight, and turn right at the park. You'll see the bank on your left.

W   Great. Thanks so much for your help!

여   실례합니다. 은행이 어디 있나요? 당좌 예금 계좌를 열어야 해서요.

남   Market Street의 끝까지 가셔서 좌회전하세요.

여   알겠어요. 그 다음에는 어떻게 하나요?

남   두 번째 길에서 우회전하세요. 학교 근처에서요.

여   그리고 그 후에는 어디로 가죠?

남   쭉 가시다가 공원에서 우회전하세요. 왼쪽에 은행이 보일 겁니다.

여   좋아요. 도와주셔서 정말 감사합니다!

18

M   What would you do if you had a million dollars? Would you buy a lot of nice things for yourself? Or would you give the money to charity? A man in New York recently faced this decision. He won a million dollars in the lottery. He was not rich before then, and the money could have helped him a lot. But he decided helping others was more important. So he donated all of his winnings to a local hospital.

남   당신에게 백만 달러가 있다면 무엇을 하시겠습니까? 당신을 위한 많은 좋은 물건들을 살 건가요? 아니면 그 돈을 자선단체에 주시겠습니까? 뉴욕의 어떤 남자는 최근에 이 결정에 직면했습니다. 그는 복권으로 백만 달러를 땄습니다. 그는 그 전에는 부자가 아니었고 그 돈은 그에게 많은 도움이 될 수 있었죠. 하지만 그는 다른 사람들을 돕는 일이 더 중요하다고 결심했습니다. 그래서 그는 당첨금 전액을 지역의 한 병원에 기부했습니다.

19

W   Are you going on the class trip, Bill?

M   I'd like to, but I don't have the money to pay.

W   Yeah, me neither. Maybe we could raise the money together.

M   Yeah, we could do a few odd jobs or something.

여   학급 수학 여행에 갈 거야, Bill?

남   그러고 싶은데 참가비를 낼 돈이 없어.

여   그래. 나도야. 어쩌면 우리 같이 돈을 모을 수도 있을 거야.

남   그래. 우리 여러 가지 작은 일을 한다거나 할 수 있을 거야.

W Hm. We could set up a car wash and charge people money.

M That's a great idea. We'll let them know it's for a good cause.

W Of course. I think they'd be happy to help us out, and get a clean car in exchange.

여 흠. 세차장을 마련하고 사람들에게 돈을 받을 수도 있어.

남 그거 좋은 생각이다. 그 사람들에게 좋은 일에 쓰일 거라고 알려주는 거야.

여 물론이지. 나는 그들이 우리를 기꺼이 도와줄 거고 그 대가로 깨끗해진 차를 얻을 거라고 생각해.

20

① **M** I have an urgent message for Mr. Park. It's very important.

   W OK. I'll give him the message right away.

② **M** Did you attend the art lecture at the museum last night?

   W Yes, I've visited the art museum many times in the past.

③ **M** I'm going to attempt to run a marathon this weekend.

   W Really? Is this your first time running a marathon?

④ **M** Will the teacher give me an extension on my essay assignment?

   W I'm not sure, but I think it wouldn't hurt to ask.

⑤ **M** I'm supposed to cook a chicken dinner for my family tonight.

   W Be careful not to overcook it. The meat will get dry.

① **남** 박 선생님에게 급히 전할 말이 있어요. 아주 중요한 겁니다.

   여 알겠어요. 바로 메시지를 전달할게요.

② **남** 어젯밤에 박물관에서 예술 강의 들었어?

   여 응. 난 예전에 그 미술관에 여러 번 가봤어.

③ **남** 나 이번 주말에 마라톤을 뛰어보려고 해.

   여 정말? 이번이 처음 마라톤 뛰는 거야?

④ **남** 선생님이 내 에세이 과제 마감을 연장해 주실까?

   여 잘 모르겠어. 그렇지만 여쭤본다고 해가 되지는 않겠지.

⑤ **남** 내가 오늘 밤에 가족들을 위해 닭고기 요리를 하기로 되어 있어.

   여 너무 익히지 않도록 주의해. 고기가 뻣뻣해질 거야.

모의고사 2회

<table>
<tr><td>01 ③</td><td>02 ①</td><td>03 ④</td><td>04 ⑤</td><td>05 ②</td><td>06 ④</td><td>07 ①</td><td>08 ③</td><td>09 ⑤</td><td>10 ②</td></tr>
<tr><td>11 ④</td><td>12 ⑤</td><td>13 ④</td><td>14 ③</td><td>15 ②</td><td>16 ③</td><td>17 ④</td><td>18 ④</td><td>19 ②</td><td>20 ②</td></tr>
</table>

01

M ① The boy is buying a new pet.
② The boy is giving away his dog.
③ The boy and his dog are visiting the vet.
④ The doctor is helping the boy.
⑤ The boy is assisting the doctor.

남 ① 소년이 새 애완동물을 사고 있다.
② 소년이 개를 다른 사람에게 주고 있다.
③ 소년과 개가 수의사를 찾아왔다.
④ 의사가 소년을 돕고 있다.
⑤ 소년이 의사를 돕고 있다.

02

M What do you like to do on the weekends, Claire?

W I love nature, so I like to go hiking and camping. What about you?

M Oh, me too! In fact, I'm going to the mountains with a hiking club next month.

W Really? Do you think I could come along?

M Of course! Do you like to mountain climb too?

W Actually, I've never tried it.

M Oh, you'll love it. We can teach you on the camping trip.

W Sounds great! I'll call you later for more details.

남 년 주말에 뭘 하는 걸 좋아하니, Claire?

여 나는 자연을 좋아해. 그래서 하이킹과 캠핑 가는 걸 좋아해. 너는 어때?

남 오, 나도 그래! 사실 난 다음 달에 하이킹 동아리와 산에 가려고 해.

여 정말? 나도 같이 가도 될 것 같아?

남 물론이지! 너 등산도 좋아하니?

여 사실 그건 한 번도 안 해봤어.

남 오, 넌 정말 좋아할 거야. 우리가 캠핑 여행에서 가르쳐 줄게.

여 재미있겠다! 나중에 너한테 전화해서 더 자세히 물어볼게.

03

[The answering machine beeps.]

M Hi, Julie. This is Max calling. I have an extra ticket to the rock concert this weekend. A friend of mine can't go. I was wondering if you would like to join me? Someone told me that you really like this band. Anyway, call me back at 555-6847. I'll be home most of the evening. Thanks, and good-bye.

[자동응답기 소리]

남 안녕, Julie. 나 Max야. 내가 이번 주말에 록 공연 표 한 장 남는 게 있어. 내 친구 한 명이 갈 수 없어. 네가 나랑 같이 가면 어떨까 하는데? 네가 이 밴드를 정말 좋아한다고 누가 그러더라고. 어쨌든 555-6847로 전화 줘. 저녁에는 거의 집에 있을 거야. 고마워, 안녕.

04

W	What do you like to do for fun, Greg?
M	Oh, I don't know. I guess I mostly read.
W	Really? I read a lot too. What's your favorite thing to read?
M	Novels, mostly. Sometimes I read short stories, too.
W	Oh. I mostly read magazines. Newspapers too. I like to learn all I can about world events.
M	Maybe we should go to the library sometime.
W	That sounds great. We can just hang out and read all day!

여	넌 뭘 하고 노는 걸 좋아해, Greg?
남	어, 잘 모르겠어. 주로 책을 읽는 것 같아.
여	정말? 나도 많이 읽어. 네가 제일 읽기 좋아하는 건 뭔데?
남	주로 소설이야. 가끔은 단편도 읽고.
여	오. 난 주로 잡지를 읽어. 신문도 읽고. 나는 세상에서 일어나는 사건에 대해 알 수 있는 모든 걸 알고 싶어.
남	어쩌면 우리 언제 도서관에 가도 좋겠다.
여	그거 좋겠네. 그냥 빈둥거리면서 하루 종일 읽을 수 있어!

05

W	Oh, I have a lot of errands to run. I'm going to the post office right now.
M	I can help, if you like. I'm not doing much today.
W	That would be so great.
M	Just tell me what you'd like me to do.
W	Well, I can take care of the grocery shopping, and also drop off the dry cleaning.
M	So what does that leave?
W	Um, do you mind cleaning up a bit? That would help a lot.
M	Sure, I'll get started now.

여	어. 처리할 일이 많아. 지금은 우체국에 가려고.
남	원한다면 내가 도와줄 수 있는데. 난 오늘 별로 할 일이 없어.
여	그러면 정말 좋겠다.
남	내가 했으면 하는 일이 뭔지 그냥 말해봐.
여	음. 식료품 사는 건 내가 할 수 있고 세탁물도 맡길 수 있어.
남	그러면 뭐가 남아?
여	음. 청소 좀 해줄래? 그러면 정말 도움이 될 것 같아.
남	물론이지. 지금 시작할게.

06

W	Welcome to City Hair Salon. What can I do for you?
M	I'd like to get a haircut, please.
W	OK. We offer several other services, if you're interested.
M	Hm, let me see… How about a hair wash to go with that?
W	Certainly. Anything else we can do for you.
M	I might as well get my face shaved while I'm here.

여	City 미용실에 오신 것을 환영합니다. 어떻게 오셨나요?
남	머리를 잘랐으면 해서요.
여	알겠습니다. 관심이 있으시다면 다른 여러 가지 서비스도 제공해 드립니다.
남	흠. 어디 보자… 머리 감는 것도 같이 하면 어떤가요?
여	물론이죠. 다른 것도 뭐든 해드릴 수 있어요.
남	제가 여기 있는 동안 면도도 받을까 해요.

W Of course. Come this way, and we'll get started.

07

M Kate was traveling abroad for the first time. Before leaving, she packed everything very carefully. She was sure she had everything she needed when she left for the airport. When she approached the ticket counter, the clerk asked for her passport. She looked everywhere, but could not find it. Had she forgotten it? Then she remembered laying it on her kitchen table at home. Her flight was about to leave, so there was no time to go home and get it. But there was no way she could travel without it. The clerk asked her, "Would you like me to move you to a later flight, ma'am?" In this situation, how would Kate respond?

여 그러세요. 이쪽으로 오시면 시작하겠습니다.

남 Kate는 처음으로 해외 여행을 하고 있었다. 떠나기 전에 그녀는 모든 것을 아주 꼼꼼하게 챙겼다. 그녀는 공항으로 떠날 때 필요한 모든 것을 챙겼다고 확신했다. 그녀가 발권대에 다가갔을 때 직원이 그녀에게 여권을 달라고 했다. 그녀는 모든 곳을 찾아보았으나 여권을 찾을 수 없었다. 잊어버린 것인가? 그때 그녀는 그것을 집의 부엌 식탁에 둔 것을 기억해냈다. 그녀의 비행기는 막 떠나려 하고 있었고 집에 가서 그것을 가져올 시간이 없었다. 하지만 여권 없이 여행할 수 있는 방법은 없었다. 직원이 그녀에게 물었다. "더 늦은 비행기로 옮겨 드릴까요?" 이런 상황에서 Kate는 어떻게 응답하겠는가?

08

[The telephone rings.]

W Hi. I'm calling to check on my car.

M We just finished with it. We had to replace a few parts.

W Really? What was wrong with it?

M Just regular maintenance. From time to time, parts just wear out.

W OK. Can I pick it up this afternoon then?

M Of course. We'll have it waiting for you.

W What was the total cost of the repairs?

M About $300, I think.

[전화벨 소리]

여 안녕하세요. 제 차에 대해서 확인하려고 전화했어요.

남 방금 끝났습니다. 부품을 몇 개 갈아야 했어요.

여 정말요? 뭐가 잘못됐었나요?

남 그냥 정기적인 유지 보수지요. 때때로 부품이 닳거든요.

여 알겠어요. 그럼 오늘 오후에 찾을 수 있나요?

남 그럼요. 대기시켜 놓겠습니다.

여 수리비 총액이 얼마였나요?

남 300달러 정도인 것 같습니다.

09

M Today, we gather to celebrate a truly amazing young man. At only 17 years old, Zac Sunderson sailed around the world, becoming the youngest person to ever do this. It was a great challenge, but Zac worked hard and achieved his dream. That's why we offer him this medal of bravery.

남 오늘 우리는 정말로 놀라운 젊은이를 축하하기 위해 모였습니다. 겨우 17살에 Zac Sunderson은 전 세계를 항해해서 이것을 한 최연소자가 되었습니다. 그것은 커다란 도전이었지만 Zac은 열심히 노력했고 꿈을 이루었습니다. 그래서 우리는 그에게 용기를 기리는 훈장을 수여하는 것입니다.

10

W I'll never forget the time we went skiing together.	여 우리가 같이 스키 타러 갔을 때를 절대 못 잊을 거야.
M Really? I don't quite remember.	남 정말? 난 잘 기억 안 나는데.
W It was ten years ago, before you knew how to ski.	여 10년 전이었어. 네가 스키 타는 법을 알기 전이었지.
M Right, I remember now. I spent the whole trip falling over on my skis.	남 맞아. 이제 기억난다. 난 여행 기간 내내 스키를 신고 넘어졌었지.
W Why did you go on the trip if you didn't know how to ski?	여 스키를 탈 줄도 모르면서 여행을 왜 간 거야?
M I wanted to impress you. But it turned out to be harder than I thought.	남 너에게 잘 보이고 싶었어. 하지만 내가 생각했던 것보다 어렵더라고.
W Well, you learned eventually. Now you love to hit the slopes.	여 음. 결국에는 배웠잖아. 이제 넌 스키 타는 걸 아주 좋아하지.

11

M What movie would you like to see, Marie?	남 어떤 영화를 보고 싶어, Marie?
W Hmm. I'm in the mood for a comedy. How about *Fun in the Sun*?	여 흠. 난 코미디를 보고 싶어. *Fun in the Sun* 어때?
M OK. We're already late for the 7:00 show, so we'll have to catch the next show, at 8:45.	남 좋아. 7시 상영에는 이미 늦었어. 그러니까 다음 상영인 8시 45분 걸 봐야겠다.
W Oh, that means the movie won't be over until after 10:00. I have to be home before then.	여 오, 그러면 영화가 10시 넘어서까지 안 끝난다는 소리잖아. 난 그 전에 집에 들어가야 해.
M I guess that means we can't see the 10:15 show, either. Hmm. We'll just have to see *The Reaper* then.	남 그렇다면 10시 15분 상영도 볼 수 없다는 말이네. 흠. 그럼 그냥 *The Reaper*를 봐야겠다.
W OK, I'm fine with a horror movie, I guess. We can see either the 7:30 show or the 8:15 show.	여 좋아, 공포 영화도 괜찮은 것 같아. 7시 30분 상영이나 8시 15분 것을 볼 수 있어.
M Let's see the earlier show.	남 더 일찍 하는 걸 보자.

12

W Building a good career certainly isn't easy. I graduated from college at age 22 and struggled for five years before I found a good job. I became an assistant at a marketing firm. After five years there, I felt like I knew a lot about advertising and marketing. So I left to start my own business. Now, ten years later, I am a successful owner of an advertising firm. It was a long journey, but it was worth it.	여 좋은 경력을 쌓는 것은 확실히 쉬운 일은 아닙니다. 저는 22살의 나이에 대학을 졸업해서 좋은 일자리를 찾기 전까지 5년 동안 힘들게 지냈습니다. 저는 마케팅 회사에서 대리급으로 일했습니다. 그곳에서 5년을 보낸 후에 저는 광고와 마케팅에 대해 많은 것을 아는 것처럼 느꼈습니다. 그래서 그곳을 떠나 제 사업을 시작했죠. 이제 10년이 지난 후 저는 한 광고 회사의 성공적인 소유주입니다. 긴 여정이었지만 그만한 가치가 있었죠.

13

M	①	The two boys are playing a game of baseball.
	②	The people are riding on a roller coaster.
	③	The boy is taking out the garbage.
	④	The kids are watching a film about animals.
	⑤	The girl is feeding her goldfish.

남	①	두 소년이 야구 경기를 하고 있다.
	②	사람들이 롤러코스터를 타고 있다.
	③	소년이 쓰레기를 내다 버리고 있다.
	④	아이들이 동물에 대한 영화를 보고 있다.
	⑤	소녀가 금붕어에게 먹이를 주고 있다.

14

W How long does it take to get to the post office?

M That depends. How do you intend to travel?

W It doesn't matter, I guess. What transportation would you suggest?

M Do you want to get there quickly?

W I am in a bit of a hurry.

M Then I'd recommend a taxi.

W That's expensive. What about the bus?

M It's cheap, but it takes longer because of all the stops.

W I would walk, but I think it's too far.

M Yes, it is. How about the subway? It's fast, direct, and cheap.

W That sounds like the best option.

여 우체국에 가는 데 얼마나 걸려?

남 경우에 따라 다르지. 어떻게 가려고 하는데?

여 상관 없을 것 같아. 어떤 교통수단을 권하겠어?

남 빨리 가고 싶니?

여 좀 급하기는 해.

남 그러면 택시를 권할게.

여 그건 비싸잖아. 버스는 어때?

남 그건 싸지만 정류장이 많아서 더 오래 걸려.

여 걸어갈 수도 있는데 너무 먼 것 같아.

남 그래, 멀어. 지하철은 어때? 그건 빠르고 직접 가고 값도 싸잖아.

여 그게 제일 좋은 방법인 것 같다.

15

W There's a poetry reading tonight at the school.

M Yeah, my teacher told me about it.

W You should really come. There's a small charge, but the money goes to charity.

M Really? That's nice. What kind of charity?

W It is to benefit the homeless in our city. They really need support from the community.

M OK, I'll be there. Maybe I'll even read some of my own poetry.

W Oh, you should! Your writing is really beautiful.

M That's nice of you to say!

여 오늘 밤에 학교에서 시 낭송회가 있어.

남 그래, 선생님이 그것에 대해 이야기해 주셨어.

여 너 꼭 와야 해. 참가비가 약간 있지만 그 돈은 자선을 위해 쓰인대.

남 정말? 그거 좋네. 어떤 종류의 자선인데?

여 우리 도시의 노숙자들을 위한 거래. 그들은 정말 지역사회의 도움을 필요로 하니까.

남 그래, 나도 갈게. 어쩌면 내 시를 몇 편 읽을 수도 있겠다.

여 오, 그래야 해! 네 글은 아주 아름다워.

남 그렇게 말해줘서 고마워!

16

M	Are you making progress in your piano lessons?
W	Yes, I'm getting better all the time.
M	Well, I'm putting together a small concert.
W	What kind of concert?
M	Just a small event where musicians from the school can show off their talents.
W	I just wrote a really beautiful piece of music.
M	Really? That's perfect! Why don't you perform it for us at the show?

남	피아노 수업은 진전이 있어?
여	응. 난 계속 더 나아지고 있어.
남	음. 내가 작은 콘서트를 열려고 하는데.
여	어떤 종류의 콘서트?
남	그냥 학생 음악가들이 그들이 재능을 뽐낼 수 있는 작은 행사야.
여	나 방금 정말 아름다운 곡을 썼는데.
남	정말? 그거 딱이다! 공연에서 우리를 위해 그 곡을 들려주지 그래?

17

W	It's been two weeks since I planted my garden in the back yard. I went to look at it today, and many of the crops are already starting to grow. I couldn't believe it! Before, I didn't even know if I had planted everything correctly. But I guess I did something right, because in just a couple more weeks I'll be picking vegetables from my very own garden!

여	내가 뒷마당에 정원을 가꾼 지 2주가 되었다. 나는 오늘 그것을 보러 갔고 농작물 중 많은 것들이 벌써 자라기 시작하고 있다. 나는 믿을 수 없었다! 전에 나는 내가 모든 것을 제대로 심었는지조차 몰랐다. 하지만 내가 뭔가를 제대로 한 것 같다. 왜냐하면 두어 주만 더 있으면 나는 나만의 정원에서 채소를 수확할 것이기 때문이다!

18

M	Did you hear the announcement at school today?
W	Yes. The principal said there would be no school play this year.
M	The drama club works too hard to have the play cancelled like that.
W	Well, it's his decision. He's the boss, you know.
M	It's a really bad decision.
W	Listen, don't take it so hard, OK? You'll have a play next year.
M	No, this is serious. Do you think I should talk to him?
W	No, not in such a bad mood. You'll get yourself into trouble. Calm down first, and then you might think about talking to the principal.

남	오늘 학교에서 공고 들었어?
여	응. 교장선생님이 올해는 학교 연극이 없을 거라고 하셨어.
남	연극 동아리는 그렇게 열심히 일했는데 그렇게 연극이 취소되어 버렸네.
여	음. 그건 그분의 결정이니까. 너도 알다시피 그분이 결정권자잖아.
남	정말 나쁜 결정이야.
여	있지. 너무 심하게 받아들이지 마. 알겠어? 내년에는 연극이 있을 거야.
남	아니야. 이건 심각해. 내가 그분이랑 이야기해 봐야 할까?
여	아니야. 그렇게 기분 나쁜 상태로는 안 돼. 넌 곤경에 처할 거야. 먼저 진정하고, 그러고 나면 교장선생님과 이야기하는 것에 대해 생각해 볼 수 있을 거야.

19

W Hey, James. Are we still studying together tomorrow afternoon?

M Yeah, I think so. I have soccer practice right after school, though. It's at 4:00.

W Oh. How about we meet after practice?

M Hm. Practice lets out at 6:00, and my mom wants me home for dinner.

W Why not study in the morning?

M I don't know. School starts at 8:00.

W Oh, it's not that early. Why don't you meet me an hour before school starts?

M OK, I guess we can try that.

여 야. James. 우리 내일 오후에 같이 공부하는 거 맞지?

남 응. 그런 것 같아. 그런데 난 학교 끝나자마자 축구 연습이 있어. 4시야.

여 오. 연습 끝나고 만나면 어때?

남 흠. 연습이 6시에 끝나는데 엄마가 나보고 집에 와서 저녁을 먹으라고 하셔서.

여 오전에 공부하면 어떨까?

남 잘 모르겠어. 학교가 8시에 시작하잖아.

여 오, 그렇게 이른 시간은 아니야. 학교 시작하기 한 시간 전에 만나면 어때?

남 그래. 그렇게 해볼 수 있겠다.

20

M I'm reading the best book right now.

W Really? What is it about?

M It's a biography about Vincent Van Gogh.

W That must be really good. I do love his paintings.

M Did you know he was kind of crazy?

W No, I didn't know that.

M Yeah, they say he cut off his own ear once. And that he talked to people who weren't there.

W My, what a troubled man. That must be why his art is so unique.

M What's more, he never sold a painting in his lifetime. People hated them!

W That's hard to believe now.

남 난 지금 최고의 책을 읽고 있어.

여 정말? 뭐에 대한 건데?

남 Vincent Van Gogh에 대한 전기야.

여 그거 정말 좋겠다. 난 그의 그림을 진짜 좋아해.

남 그가 좀 미쳤었던 거 알았어?

여 아니. 그건 몰랐어.

남 그랬어. 그는 한번은 자기 귀를 잘랐대. 그리고 그 자리에 없는 사람들에게 이야기를 했대.

여 와. 정말 문제가 많은 사람이었구나. 그래서 그의 예술이 그렇게 독특한 걸 거야.

남 더 놀라운 건, 그가 평생 동안 그림을 한 점도 팔지 못했다는 거야. 사람들이 작품들을 싫어했대!

여 그건 지금은 믿기 힘들다.

모의고사 3회

01 ②	02 ③	03 ⑤	04 ③	05 ②	06 ④	07 ②	08 ④	09 ①	10 ④
11 ①	12 ④	13 ⑤	14 ⑤	15 ②	16 ③	17 ②	18 ③	19 ③	20 ③

01

① W I'm a bit disappointed in your test scores, Miguel.

M I'm sorry. I feel pretty ashamed about them.

② W I'm very proud of you for scoring so well on the test.

M Thanks, Ms. Green. I couldn't be happier about it.

③ W Are you sure you don't want to study together?

M No thanks. I'm on my way to basketball practice.

④ W What do you like to do for fun, Miguel?

M I mostly like to read novels and magazines in my spare time.

⑤ W Can you give me some tips on studying?

M Sure. Come into my classroom and we'll talk.

① 여 난 네 시험 점수에 좀 실망했다. Miguel.

남 죄송해요. 그것에 대해 정말 부끄러워요.

② 여 시험에서 그렇게 좋은 점수를 받다니 네가 자랑스럽구나.

남 감사합니다. Green 선생님. 저도 정말 기뻐요.

③ 여 정말 같이 공부하고 싶지 않아?

남 고맙지만 사양할게. 난 농구 연습하러 가는 길이야.

④ 여 넌 뭘 하고 노는 걸 좋아해. Miguel?

남 난 주로 한가할 때 소설이랑 잡지를 읽는 걸 좋아해.

⑤ 여 공부에 대해서 조언을 좀 주실 수 있으세요?

남 그럼. 내 교실로 와서 얘기하자꾸나.

02

M Are you going to the fair this weekend, Pam?

W Are you serious? I never miss the fair when it's in town.

M Would you like to go together on Saturday?

W Oh, I promised my family that I'd go out for dinner with them.

M Well, we can just spend the day there. You'll be free to do what you like that night.

W That sounds like a good plan to me.

M So will I see you there?

남 이번 주말에 박람회에 가니. Pam?

여 농담하는 거야? 박람회가 열릴 때면 난 한 번도 놓치지 않잖아.

남 토요일에 같이 갈래?

여 오, 난 가족들이랑 저녁 먹으러 같이 나가기로 약속했어.

남 음. 그럼 낮에 거기서 시간을 보내면 되겠네. 그날 저녁에는 뭘 하든 자유롭게 해.

여 그거 좋은 계획처럼 들린다.

남 그럼 거기서 볼까?

03

W A large weather system is moving across the country this week. Temperatures are expected to be lower all over the country. This will bring strong storms to the southern region. Some places may even experience tornadoes and large hail. In the north, people should prepare for large amounts of snow.

여 대형 일기계가 이번 주에 전국을 가로지를 예정입니다. 기온은 전국에 걸쳐 낮을 것으로 예상됩니다. 이것은 남부 지역에 강한 폭풍우를 가져올 것입니다. 일부 지역들은 토네이도와 큰 우박을 경험할 수도 있습니다. 북쪽에 사는 주민들은 많은 양의 눈에 대비해야 합니다.

04

M Thanks for shopping at Fresh Market. Did you find what you were looking for?

W Yes, and I must say, your sales are great.

M That's good to hear. Are you ready to check out, ma'am?

W Yes, thank you. Here are a pound of apples.

M OK. And I see a pound of pears as well, right?

W Yes, that's right. And a half-pound of plums.

M OK. And how many oranges do you have there?

W Five oranges, thank you. What's the total price?

남 Fresh Market을 이용해 주셔서 감사합니다. 찾으시는 물건을 찾으셨나요?

여 네. 그리고 이 말을 해야겠는데. 파는 물건들이 아주 좋네요.

남 반가운 말씀이네요. 계산할 준비가 되셨나요?

여 네. 고마워요. 여기 사과 1파운드가 있어요.

남 네. 그리고 배 1파운드도 보이네요. 맞나요?

여 네. 맞아요. 그리고 자두 반 파운드요.

남 알겠습니다. 그리고 거기 오렌지는 몇 개 갖고 계신가요?

여 오렌지 5개예요. 감사합니다. 총 금액이 얼마죠?

05

W What do you do for fun, Mark?

M I like extreme sports, like skateboarding and snowboarding

W Me too! In fact, I just got back from a BMX bike competition.

M That sounds awesome. I'd love to go to one sometime.

W Haven't you ever seen it live?

M No, I'm afraid I haven't.

W Oh, you must. It's so exciting.

여 넌 재미로 뭘 하니. Mark?

남 나는 익스트림 스포츠를 좋아해. 스케이트보드나 스노우보드 말이야.

여 나도야! 사실 난 BMX 자전거 대회에서 방금 돌아왔어.

남 그거 멋지다. 나도 언제 정말 가보고 싶은데.

여 직접 본 적 없어?

남 어. 없어.

여 오. 꼭 봐야 해. 정말 신나.

06

M What are you doing this summer, Eve?

W I'm volunteering to help the homeless.

M Really? That's very noble of you.

남 이번 여름에 뭐 해. Eve?

여 노숙자들을 돕는 일에 자원봉사를 하려고.

남 정말? 아주 훌륭하다.

W Yeah, I just love supporting good causes.	**여** 응. 난 그냥 좋은 명분을 지지하는 게 좋아.
M Maybe you should work for a charity one day.	**남** 어쩌면 넌 언젠가 자선단체에서 일해야 할지도 모르겠다.
W I plan to do that after university. I want to study social services.	**여** 대학을 졸업한 후에 그러려고 계획하고 있어. 사회 복지를 공부하고 싶어.
M I'm confident that you'd do a great job.	**남** 넌 아주 잘 해낼 거라고 확신해.

07

M Did you see the new horror movie this weekend?	**남** 이번 주말에 그 새로 나온 공포 영화 봤어?
W Yes, I did. It was a lot of fun, I guess.	**여** 응. 봤어. 꽤 재미있었던 것 같아.
M You guess? You mean you didn't love it?	**남** 그런 것 같다고? 아주 좋지는 않았다는 말이야?
W It could've been better. The acting was terrible, for one thing.	**여** 더 나을 수 있었어. 한 가지로 연기가 형편없었어.
M What about the story? Wasn't it scary?	**남** 내용은 어때? 무섭지 않았어?
W Oh yes, I was definitely scared. But the actors ruined the movie for me.	**여** 오, 무서웠어. 난 확실히 겁에 질렸어. 하지만 내가 보기엔 배우들이 영화를 망쳤어.
M Well, they can't all be classics, I guess.	**남** 음. 모든 영화가 고전일 수는 없으니까.

08

W I'm so excited to be here. I've looked forward to this exhibit.	**여** 여기 와서 너무 신난다. 이 전시를 손꼽아 기다려왔어.
M Me too. I hear there are a lot of famous paintings in the collection.	**남** 나도야. 이번 컬렉션에 유명한 작품이 많다고 들었어.
W There's a sculpture by Rodin, too.	**여** Rodin의 조각도 있어.
M I wonder when the next tour begins?	**남** 다음 투어는 언제 시작하는지 모르겠네?
W I don't know. Would you like me to ask an attendant?	**여** 나도 몰라. 직원에게 물어볼까?
M No, we'll just wait here. The gallery is probably crowded right now anyway.	**남** 아니야. 그냥 여기서 기다리지 뭐. 어쨌든 지금은 전시장이 아마 붐빌 거야.

09

M Dear Manager,	**남** 지배인님 귀하

I recently visited your store and had a terrible experience. I wanted to buy a computer, but I couldn't find any workers to help me. In addition, the cashier was very rude. I don't know if this is the way you always do business, but if you ask me, it's a terrible approach.

저는 최근에 귀 매장을 방문했는데 아주 좋지 않은 경험을 했습니다. 저는 컴퓨터를 사고 싶었지만 저를 도와줄 직원을 찾을 수 없었습니다. 게다가 계산원은 아주 무례했습니다. 항상 이런 식으로 장사를 하시는 건지는 모르겠습니다만 제 생각을 물으신다면 아주 좋지 않은 방식입니다.

10

W Mr. Brown, you had a call while you were
out.

M Who was it?

W A woman named Lisa Strong called.

M Oh, yes. We have a dinner date this week.

W Yes, she wanted to remind you that it is
Tuesday at 7:00.

M Yes, I remember that. At the Sushi Palace,
right?

W That's correct, sir. She asked you to call
her back as soon as you can.

M Thank you for passing along the message.

여 Brown 씨. 나가 계신 동안 전화가 한 통 왔어요.

남 누구였나요?

여 Lisa Strong이라는 여자분이 전화하셨어요.

남 오. 그래요. 이번 주에 저녁 식사 데이트가 있어요.

여 네. 그게 화요일 7시라는 걸 상기시켜 드리고 싶어했어요.

남 그래요. 기억해요. Sushi Palace에서 맞죠?

여 맞습니다. 가능하실 때 바로 전화 달라고 하셨어요.

남 메시지를 전달해줘서 고마워요.

11

M Did you go to your hometown for the
holidays?

W Yes, I did. That place has really changed
since my childhood.

M Why? What is it like now?

W There are a lot more buildings, shops,
malls, things like that.

M Well, what was it like before?

W It was a really small town, with mostly just
houses and a few businesses.

M Everything has to change, I suppose.

남 연휴에 고향에 갔었어?

여 응. 그랬어. 그곳은 내가 어렸을 때 이후로 정말 변했어.

남 왜? 지금은 어떤데?

여 건물. 상점. 쇼핑몰 같은 것들이 훨씬 많아졌어.

남 음. 전에는 어땠는데?

여 정말 작은 마을이었어. 주로 그냥 집들이랑 몇 개의 가
게만 있었지.

남 모든 것은 변해야 하는 거겠지.

12

W May I have your attention, please? I'd
like to talk to you about applying for college.
Many of you will be thinking of that soon.
Remember, it can be very hard to get into a
big university. Don't be disappointed if you
get turned down a few times. Wherever you
go to school, you will get the education that
you want and need. So try not to get too
stressed out about it.

여 잠깐 주목해 주시겠습니까? 여러분께 대학에 지원하는
것에 대해 말씀드리고 싶습니다. 여러분 중 많은 경우에 그
것에 대해 곧 생각하게 될 것입니다. 기억하세요. 큰 대학에
들어가는 것은 아주 어려울 수 있습니다. 몇 번 거절당한다
고 해서 실망하지 마세요. 어디로 학교를 가든지 여러분은
여러분이 원하고 필요로 하는 교육을 받게 될 것입니다. 그
러니 그것에 대해 너무 스트레스 받지 않도록 하세요.

13

M I've decided to enter the school talent
competition.

W Really? What talent will you show off?

남 나 학교 장기자랑 대회에 나가기로 결심했어.

여 정말? 어떤 장기를 보여줄 건데?

M I'm a pretty good singer. I think I'll sing a song.

W Is this your first time singing in public?

M Yes, I've never done it before now.

W You know, you will have to compete against a lot of really talented people.

M I know. But I can't win if I don't try, can I?

W I'll keep my fingers crossed for you!

남 난 노래를 아주 잘 해. 노래를 부를까 해.

여 사람들 앞에서 노래하는 게 이번이 처음이니?

남 응. 지금까지 한 번도 해본 적이 없어.

여 있잖아. 넌 정말 재능 있는 많은 사람들과 맞서 경쟁해야 할 거야.

남 알아. 하지만 시도해 보지 않으면 이길 수도 없는 거 아냐?

여 널 위해 행운을 빌어줄게!

14

W I love looking at these old photographs! Do you remember this one?

M Of course! How could I forget?

W It was our first family vacation. We didn't have much money, so we just drove down to the coast.

M I have a lot of great memories from that trip. We just relaxed on the sand and played in the ocean.

W We saw a lot of colorful fish near the shore, too.

M Yeah, that was neat. We should really go back sometime.

여 난 이 오래된 사진들을 보는 게 정말 좋아! 이거 기억나?

남 당연하지! 어떻게 잊겠어?

여 우리가 처음으로 가족 여행을 갔던 때였지. 우린 돈이 별로 없어서 그냥 해안으로 운전해 갔어.

남 난 그 여행에 대한 좋은 추억이 많아. 우린 그냥 모래사장에 누워서 쉬고 바다에서 놀았지.

여 물가에서 알록달록한 물고기도 많이 보고 말이야.

남 맞아. 멋졌어. 언제 다시 꼭 가봐야 해.

15

M I only have one goal for when I grow up. It's something I've wanted to do all my life. I first became interested in movies when I was a kid. And I started making short films at home. One day, hopefully, I'll be able to make a real movie of my own, as a film director. That's my biggest wish for the future.

남 저는 장래의 목표가 딱 하나 있습니다. 제가 평생 하고 싶었던 것입니다. 저는 어린 아이였을 때 영화에 처음 관심을 갖게 되었습니다. 그리고 집에서 짧은 영화를 만들기 시작했죠. 언젠가는 영화 감독으로서 저만의 진짜 영화를 만들 수 있기를 바랍니다. 그게 미래에 대한 저의 가장 큰 바람입니다.

16

[The telephone rings.]

W What are you doing today, Mike?

M I'm gathering up things to donate to charity.

W Me too! What kinds of things are you giving away?

M Anything, really. Food, clothing, toys for

[전화벨 소리]

여 오늘 뭐 해, Mike?

남 자선단체에 기부할 것들을 모으고 있어.

여 나도야! 어떤 것들을 기부하려고 해?

남 어떤 것이든. 음식. 옷. 아이들을 위한 장난감. 어떤 사람

kids. Things that some people just can't
afford.

W Why don't I come over and help? I can
bring some things to donate as well.

M That'd be great! We can take them
downtown to the donation center together.

W OK. I'll see you in a little while.

들이 돈이 없어서 살 수 없는 물건들 말이야.

여 내가 가서 도우면 어떨까? 나도 기부할 것들을 좀 가져
갈 수 있어.

남 그러면 정말 좋겠다! 그것들을 시내에 있는 기부 센터에
같이 가져가면 되겠다.

여 좋아. 조금 이따 봐.

17

M I'm writing to complain about an article in
last year's newspaper. You wrote an article
that praised electric cars. However, I say
they are not as good for the environment as
some people think. After all, the cars get their
electricity from power plants that create all
kinds of pollution. I think we should do more
to develop clean energy. Then we can talk
about electric cars.

남 저는 지난해 신문에 난 어떤 기사에 대해 불평하기 위해
이 글을 씁니다. 당신은 전기 자동차를 찬양하는 기사를 썼습
니다. 하지만 그것들은 일부 사람들이 생각하는 만큼 환경에
좋지 않습니다. 따지고 보면 그 차들은 온갖 공해를 만들어내
는 발전소로부터 전기를 얻습니다. 저는 우리가 깨끗한 에너
지를 개발하기 위해 더 많은 노력을 해야 한다고 생각합니다.
그리고 나서 전기 자동차에 대해 이야기할 수 있습니다.

18

W I can't decide how many steaks to buy for
the party.

M Well, how many people are coming?

W There are ten guests coming over. So,
should I only buy ten steaks?

M What if someone wants a second serving?

W You're right, I might need extras. What do
you think about twice as many steaks as
guests?

M That might be too much. How about five
extra steaks instead?

W OK, I think that will turn out fine.

여 파티에 쓸 스테이크를 몇 개나 사야 할지 모르겠어.

남 음. 사람들이 얼마나 오는데?

여 올 손님이 열 명 있어. 그러니까 스테이크를 10개만
사면 될까?

남 누군가가 한 번 더 먹고 싶어하면 어떻게 해?

여 당신 말이 맞아. 여유분이 필요할지 몰라. 손님 수보다
두 배 많은 수의 스테이크를 사는 건 어때?

남 그건 너무 많을 수 있어. 대신에 스테이크를 5개 더
사는 게 어때?

여 좋아. 그게 좋을 것 같네.

19

W Mike, did you do your homework?

M No, I'm going to do it after I meet my
friends.

W You know the rules. No going out until
homework is done.

M But I told my friends I'd meet them at the
mall!

W It doesn't matter. Your schoolwork comes

여 Mike. 너 숙제 했니?

남 아니오, 친구들 만나고 나서 하려고요.

여 너 규칙 알잖아. 숙제 다 하기 전까지 외출하지 않기.

남 하지만 친구들한테 쇼핑몰에서 보자고 말했단 말이에
요!

여 상관 없어. 학교 일이 우선이야.

first.

M But why? There's plenty of time to do it later.

W I'm not going to argue about this. Would you rather be grounded for a week?

M No, ma'am. I'm going to do my homework now.

W That's better. I want to see it before you leave.

남 하지만 왜요? 나중에 할 시간이 많잖아요.

여 이것에 대해서 말다툼하지 않을 거야. 일주일 동안 외출 금지 당하고 싶니?

남 아뇨. 지금 숙제 할게요.

여 좀 낫구나. 네가 나가기 전에 그것[숙제]을 봐야겠다.

20

① **M** Do you know why Jack didn't show up to the meeting?

   W He had to leave early because of an emergency.

② **M** Do you remember the time I cooked you dinner?

   W How could I forget? The food was terrible!

③ **M** How long have you worked for this company?

   W I had several different jobs before this one.

④ **M** How long does it take to drive downtown?

   W In this traffic, it could take an hour or more.

⑤ **M** Can you recommend a good restaurant for dinner?

   W My favorite is the Mexican restaurant downtown.

① 남 Jack이 왜 회의에 참석하지 않았는지 알아요?

   여 급한 일이 있어서 조퇴해야 했어요.

② 남 내가 널 위해 저녁을 요리했을 때 기억해?

   여 어떻게 잊겠어? 음식이 형편없었는데!

③ 남 이 회사에서 얼마나 오래 일하셨나요?

   여 이 회사에 오기 전에 여러 가지 일을 했어요.

④ 남 시내로 운전해 가는 데 얼마나 걸리나요?

   여 이 교통량에서는 한 시간이나 그보다 더 걸릴 수 있어요.

⑤ 남 저녁을 먹을 좋은 식당을 추천해 주실래요?

   여 제가 제일 좋아하는 곳은 시내에 있는 멕시코 식당이에요.

센치한 Listening 길들이기

중학 영어 내신 만점을 향한 길들이기 시리즈

- 센치한 Listening 길들이기 총 6권
- 도도한 Reading 길들이기 총 6권
- 까칠한 Grammar 길들이기 총 6권